BROKEN CHAINS

~

LADY KADIJATU GRACE AHENE

JB TREMONT, LLC
Delaware

Lady Kadijatu Grace Ahene

Published by JB Tremont, LLC
Glenside, Pennsylvania, 19038, U.S.A.

Library of Congress Control Number: 2016908159

ISBN 13 978-0-692-66862-7
ISBN 10 0-692-66862-4

Printed in the United States of America

Edited by: JB Tremont
Cover design by: Marvic Olu Jones, Marvic Studio Productions

www.jbtremont.com

MY TESTIMONY

Jesus heals a woman that has been bleeding for 12 years. This consistent bleeding (causes unknown) is considered "unclean" in her community. As Jesus walks through the town to go and heal a young girl, the bleeding woman touches the hem of Jesus' garment. When Jesus turns and sees the woman, He simply explains to her that by her faith, she is healed. It is amazing that just by her reaching out in faith results   in her being healed of 12 years' worth of bleeding, shame, embarrassment, rejection, scrutiny, and who knows what other struggles she faced. All it takes is a little bit of faith and God can make the impossible, possible.

For many years I too struggled with pain. Not physical pain, but more mental and emotional pain. I guess I was trying to fill voids that I just did not know how to fill or if they could be filled. Being an only child of my mother, not knowing who my father was and not having a relationship with him, I was lost. For as long as I can remember, I have always been the bold, friendly type who kept friends everywhere I could find them, except I loved my privacy and was not really familiar with saying "NO" to people. My longing to fill those mysterious voids in my life led me to, what I now see as, a road of self-pity, and self-destruction.

As a teenager, once I found out that my talent in dancing and singing made boys attracted to me, I immediately thought I found a way to fill the voids of wanting to be wanted. Not only in boys, but in anyone that gave me their ears satisfied me for the moment. I don't know what it was about the opposite sex being attracted to me, but I know I enjoyed it.

My mother and her sisters were strict, so of course that meant everything had to be secretive. The rebellion was so exciting. Because I was never listened to, my voice was never heard. Coming from a family with twenty (20) first cousins, I felt like an outcast. I rebelled by lying to have my way; I rebelled so that I could be heard.

Eventually, this became a pattern for me, but I was so used to it. I felt I couldn't stop. Saying "no" became harder and harder, because I didn't know any better; I felt emptier than before. The boys I invited into my most personal space, left with my purity, my youth, my dignity, pieces of my already broken heart, and left me even more confused and hurt than ever. My desire for love and attention, coupled with my rebellion, led to trust issues. The heartbreak I experienced from family and friends (I was on the receiving and giving end of heartbreak), felt like brick walls that I had built around the surviving pieces of my heart. These pieces included indecision, shame, guilt, fear, and unworthiness. Here's my story.....

Lady Kadijatu Grace Ahene

LIFE'S A JOURNEY

In life we all get to a point where we just want a change. We get tired of doing things the same way, and getting the same results. I know I was. I was tired of carrying the same baggage that weighed me down for so long. So at age twenty-five (25), I began to find ways to "change." I picked up a few "self-help" books, and did some internet research on self-improvement. The words in those books made me feel good, but I'm pretty sure it was the anti-depressants and anxiety medicine I was prescribed to suppress my deepest secrets which made me feel better.

Soon after, the soul-searching/self-repairing research led me to spiritual books, articles, pastors' sermons, and the Bible. I began reading and praying. I grew up in church; I knew who God was, but I realized that to "know of God" and to "know God" are two different things. I studied the Bible more deeply, and my prayers became a little bit stronger.

I remember my strongest prayer ever, was the eve of my twenty-fifth birthday when I asked God, "If this is life, then take my life already." I was not thinking of my mother, anyone or anything else around me. The rejection and humiliation from every con artist had me in a cage; I felt like I couldn't get out of. So, I began to worship God and then I cried from the deepest part of my broken soul, asking God to help me. I asked him to make me new, to restore my joy, to have His way, to forgive me for bad decisions, to remove the pain I carried for so long and the anger that was created in the process. I cried for so long...I just wanted to start over.

That moment was the moment my life begins to change for the better, for the best! God heard my cry. I asked, I received; I sought, I found Him; I knocked and He invited me in and taught me about His unconditional love. Now during this change, I felt His love, but also experienced more hate from my surroundings. There were spiritual attacks everywhere: from dreams, to seeing things physically, to hearing voices that would tell me to drive into ongoing traffic. I also craved a man's touch; after which I felt so dirty about myself. I couldn't say no to men; it was like the voices would tell me, "If you say no you are a bad person." Mind you, at this time, I had just a small piece of faith to give, because I thought I lost it all. But I cried out to Him, and God soon begin working in my life.

I was married to someone who was also lost in his own life's journey. We both didn't know how to help each other. It is true when it is said, cast your burdens unto Jesus that He will see you through. Getting married at twenty-five I thought would bring an end to me being lost; I felt that was the only way I could be complete. But oh no, I jumped from a frying pan into the fire. I was being emotionally abused! My hair was falling out; I would pass out and wake up in the ER. My diagnosis was high-risk depression.

I felt the emotional abuse was beyond repair. But God favored me! He set me on the rock to stand; He turned me in to an eagle, so now I can say "MY CHAINS ARE GONE!!!"

God has been so good to me, Jesus died for me, and the Holy Spirit is always here to guide me and intercede for me. God put it on my heart to share this story, this testimony... MY Story, MY

Testimony. I was afraid, but He kept reminding me that my past does not define who He has called me to be. God has taken the pain of my past and uses it to do His will (Genesis 50:20). He told me to <u>not</u> be ashamed to tell of His goodness (Romans 1:16). If He Did It for Me, He Can Do the Same for You!

Our purpose on earth is to be servants of God, to honor and obey Him. He wants us to share His Word, and lead others to Him, by being witnesses of His Grace and Mercy. Through Jesus Christ we have been forgiven and we can be made new if we believe that Jesus Christ is Lord and accept Him as our Savior (John 1: 12-13). I know that I have changed because a lot of the things that used to interest me, do not interest me; things that once made me sad, mad or angry, don't bother me; and I can smile and it's genuine.

But I am human, I still mess up. The difference is I've learned the importance of repentance. I will be honest though, the change is not easy, but I know that it is necessary. I just remind myself that Jesus suffered way more than any of us to give us a chance of receiving eternal life despite our sinful nature, and this is what makes the struggle of change worth it. This new life that I received is no longer self-centered; my life is all about God (Romans 7:4).

Just seek God! To Him it does not matter what you've done, what you haven't done, what you've been through, or how you seek Him. He just wants us to seek Him and have faith. He can make the impossible, possible. God has the power to heal and restore you.

Love,

Lady Kadijatu Grace Ahene

Table of Contents

Lady Kadijatu Grace Ahene

SAYING NO TO SELF-PITY

The bread of idleness (gossip, discontent, and self-pity) she (the virtuous woman) will not eat.

Proverbs 31:27

I recently went through some difficulties that got me so discouraged that I found myself wrestling with feelings of self-pity. Years ago, I might have played some sad songs and cried my eyes out, deriving a sort of perverse satisfaction from my misery. But this time, I prayed and asked the Lord to help me resist these negative emotions. That's when He reminded me about some teaching I heard years ago about self-pity. I once heard a godly man say, "God is concerned about your hurt, but He doesn't want YOU concerned about it." This man went on to say that the reason self-pity is so destructive is that pride is at the root of it, and it causes us to focus too much on ourselves. I looked "self-pity" up in the dictionary and found the following definition: "A self-indulgent dwelling on one's own sorrows or misfortunes." (Women's

Empowerment Summit 2015, "My Sister's Keeper Group", Grace International Ministry)

Psychiatrists have an interesting name for people who habitually indulge in self-pity: it's "injustice collector." These are the folks who are constantly dwelling on their hurts and hardships - whether real or imagined - and they enjoy thinking about them and talking about them. They lovingly collect and number each and every offense that others commit against them, and they search out people who will sympathize with them and commiserate with them. All this keeps the focus on themselves, which is what they want most. But this isn't God's way. He instructs us to walk in the God-kind of love, which is "not self-seeking," and which "keeps no record of wrongs." (1 Corinthians 13:5) This is not to say that we should ignore or deny when we're being mistreated, but that we should take constructive action to see that we are treated with proper respect, or remove ourselves from harm's way, rather than sit idly by, feeling sorry for ourselves.

Self-pity isn't just nonproductive, it's destructive. It can lead to bitterness, unforgiveness, and resentment. It doesn't bring people together, it divides them. And these are some of the reasons why Satan works so hard to get us to focus on our wounds, rather than the cure - which is the love and wisdom of God.

Throughout the pages of the Bible, God tells us again and again that He wants us to bring our hurts and sorrows to Him, so that HE can comfort us. He not only wants to be our Comforter, but our Vindicator. (Psalm 135:14) If we let Him, He will defend us and fight our battles for us, leading us to victory every time. He tells us in His Word: "I, the Lord, love justice. I hate robbery and wrongdoing. I will faithfully reward my people for their suffering..." (Isaiah 61:8)

A good antidote for self-pity is Forgiveness. As we forgive those who offend us, we can let go of our negative emotions and ill-feelings toward others, and we can receive the comfort and healing that can only come from God. Scripture says: "In all their suffering He also suffered, and He personally rescued them. In His love and mercy, He redeemed them. He lifted them up and carried them through all the years." (Isaiah 63:9) God hurts when we hurt, and He wants to be our Deliverer. But we can block His efforts to comfort and rescue us when we insist on holding onto our feelings of resentment, bitterness, and forgiveness. As we choose to forgive, we open the door to God's involvement, and all the blessings and provisions that entails.

Another good antidote for self-pity is Thankfulness. The Bible says: "Thank God in everything, no matter what the circumstances may be, be thankful and give thanks, for this is the will of God for you [who are] in Christ Jesus." (1 Thessalonians 5:18) No matter what is going on in our lives, we always have reason to give thanks to God and praise Him. Nothing is more offensive to God than our dwelling on our misfortunes and losses, and neglecting to recognize and enumerate all of the blessings He bestows on us daily.

Helen Keller said, "Self-pity is our worst enemy and if we yield to it, we can never do anything good in the world." We have been chosen by God, not just to live eternally with Him in heaven, but to make a difference for Him while we're still here on earth.

Let's not allow self-pity to neutralize all the good we can do in this world in the name of Jesus. [1]

> **Prayer**: Lord, please alert me whenever I begin to feel sorry for myself. Keep me from being overly-sensitive and self-absorbed, and teach me to bring all of my hurts and hardships straight to You. When I do, heal and comfort me the way that only You can. Give me the grace I need to forgive others quickly and thoroughly, and to praise You in all things. Thank You that as I resist self-pity in the power of Your Spirit, I will be rewarded by a gracious and grateful God!

When things go wrong, instead of responding appropriately, many indulge in loneliness or despair until it becomes a melancholy mindset, a distorted way of thinking, seeing, and feeling.

---

[1] David Brandon and Associates, My Pocket Prayer Partner for Women, (New York: Howard Books, 2007) pp. 42-43

Many times, such people feed their sadness by becoming dependent on their despondency to provide them with a sick sort of comfort. Just as a famine can lead a person to make a more intense search for food, one wallowing in self-pity must strive to find a cure for this morose state of mind (II Corinthians 2:11).

When times get hard, those who have sunk into apathy curl up in self-pity. Conversely, the faithful patiently and quietly wait, trusting God to make things right in His perfect time. Those who pity themselves because of the circumstances of their lives fail to see God at work in them, while the faithful understand that God always has their best and eternal interests at heart. In this final Bible study in the series on overcoming, we will analyze the sin of self-pity.

1. What is the difference between pity and self-pity? James 5:11 James 5:11; Job 19:21-22; Proverbs 19:17; Psalm 103:13; I Peter 3:8.

Self-Deception

In studying the seven churches of Revelation 2-3, we have found that all have one thing in common: the need to overcome. Some eras receive more chastening and harsher criticism than others do, yet Christ admonishes even the "best" or least criticized to overcome. This suggests that all these churches fall short of God's standard of Holiness. All lack faith, hope, love, obedience, dedication, and responsiveness, among other aspects of character. All still produce the works of the flesh, man's carnal nature and selfishness.

Since our Savior directly instructs all the churches to overcome, this series of Bible study addresses this vital matter. We will first look into the various impediments to overcoming—the sinful attitudes and conditions that hold us back. To begin, we need to see what part self-deception plays in concealing our true spiritual condition from us. If we hide our sins even from ourselves, we will never work to overcome them!

1. How can members of God's church be completely deceived about their true standing with God? Ezekiel 28:14-18;

Revelation 12:9; II John 7; Jeremiah 2:21-23; 17:9; James 1:22-24.

Self-Justification

In the last issue, we examined the first deterrent to overcoming: self-deception. The heart is deceitful above all things, and it first fools the self! In the end time, at least two of the seven church eras of Revelation 3 are totally self-deceived, so we must look honestly into the mirror of the law of liberty, God's Word, and not forget to remove the "dirt" we see in ourselves.

In the children's fable, "The Emperor's New Clothes,"[2] the monarch's clothing is invisible, entirely a figment of his imagination. The emperor's view of himself has no substance in truth. He walks about as if clothed in the finest raiment, but in reality he exposes his true condition — nakedness. Similarly, self-righteousness, a root of Laodiceanism (Numbers 15:22), is a most difficult sin to recognize since it is a matter of attitude rather than action. It is complacency in its worse form, because it involves regarding oneself as more

---

[2] Andersen, H C, and Virginia L. Burton. *The Emperor's New Clothes*. Boston: Houghton Mifflin Co, 1949. Print.

virtuous than others despite the reality of a deficient spiritual condition.

This lie was introduced first by Lucifer out of his rebellious attitude. Regarding Satan, Ezekiel writes, "Your heart was lifted up because of your beauty; you corrupted your wisdom for the sake of your splendor" (Ezekiel 28:17). He became greater and more righteous in his own eyes than his Creator. So also being righteous in our own eyes spiritually exposes our sin to God. This Bible study will analyze this dangerous impediment to overcoming.

1. Does a self-righteous person see his sin for what it is? Job 32:1-2; 33:9; Psalm 19:12-13; Isaiah 46:12; 64:6; Revelation 3:17.

2. When our sins are uncovered, what is our normal first reaction? Is it common to man? Genesis 3:10-13; 4:9; Acts 5:1-11.

Self-Will

A sixteenth-century doctor, Thomas Fuller, once said, "Beware of no man more than thyself." In our efforts to overcome, we find this statement painfully true. Self-will is part of our human nature and always strives to make self the center of its own universe. In this selfish manner, our self-will desires to pull God from His throne and deny others justice and mercy to advance its own ambition. This sin is both dangerous and destructive.

A major theme of the Bible shows what God has done to save man from disasters that have overtaken him, because of his self-will. In addition, it reveals man's persistent refusal to recognize God's greater will and its amazing benefits when followed. Man's own stubbornness is keeping him from lasting peace, health and prosperity! This Bible study will examine this presumptuous obstruction to overcoming.

1. What are some of the harsher characteristics of self-will? Genesis 49:5-7.

Comment: "Self-will" occurs only here in the Old Testament. In his curse on Simeon and Levi, Jacob says that in their self-will, they "digged down a wall" (KJV), or "hamstrung an ox" (NKJV). Their vengeful, violent acts against Shechem cause Jacob to pronounce a curse on their anger, because it manifested itself in fierceness and cruelty. As a result, the tribes of Simeon and Levi, given no inheritance, are scattered throughout Israel.

   2. Can ambition be another form of self-will? Isaiah 14:13-14; Genesis 11:4; II Samuel 15:1-6.

Self-Denial

The phrase "deny himself", so characteristic of the life of a true Christian, is found in Scripture in only one of Jesus' sayings to His disciples: "If anyone desires to come after Me, let him deny himself, and take up his cross, and follow Me." (Matthew 16:24; see also Mark 8:34; Luke 9:23) The Greek verb translated, deny, also means "to say no." Luke's version of Jesus' teaching adds that we should do this daily. But what does Jesus mean that a person must deny himself? We continue in this Bible study series on impediments to overcoming by exploring self-denial, a "must-have" key to Christian growth.

1. What must we deny ourselves? Matthew 16:24-26; Romans 12:1-2; I Thessalonians 4:1-8; I Peter 4:2; I John 2:15-17.

Comment: Jesus calls upon His followers to reject the natural human inclination toward self. The first step is to submit and surrender to God our will, our affections, our bodies, and our lives. Our own pleasures and happiness can no longer be primary goals. Instead, we must be willing to renounce all and lay down our lives, if required.

for the lusts of men," meaning we should no longer
pursue wrong desires. Are we willing to forsake all,
to give up everything including our lives? Our
Christian duty is to deny our lust of the flesh.

2. Does the New Testament refer to self-denial
   in other ways? Matthew 10:38; Luke 14:33;
   Galatians 5:24; Ephesians 4:22-24;
   Colossians 3:5-10.

Comment: Christ calls us to take up our cross and
follow His example. This call is not so much a call
to martyrdom, as a command to deny self, or
crucify the flesh, even to the point of death. We
must be prepared to die, if that is where the course
of events leads, but in most cases it is not so much
literal martyrdom as it is to have the attitude of
self-denial: that is, willing to give up all. Christ's
disciples live to serve God, not self. Paul
admonishes us to put off our former conduct and
put to death our sinful actions.

Self-Surrender

Everyone struggles between the negative impulses of self-seeking and self-defense on the one hand, and the positive, unselfish impulses toward self-denial and self-surrender on the other. All religions maintain some concept of surrender of self to deity, ranging from heathen fanaticism to self-sacrifice for the holiest aims and achievements. But what distinguishes righteous from unrighteous surrender? Is it knowing the truth that sets us free to worship and surrender in faith to the one true God?

A Christian's life can be described as a life of both self-surrender and self-development. To some, this may seem contradictory, but only when we surrender self-will can we realize our human potential. We must give up what our carnal nature holds dear to take hold of something greater, spiritual and eternal. In this Bible study, we will survey this noblest of human virtues — self-surrender.

1. Has man from earliest times been required to surrender himself? Genesis 2:24; 3:16; 12:1; 22:1-8; Hebrews 11:23-27.

Comment: The Old Testament teaches self-surrender in the account of Adam and Eve. Each is given to the other and both are to surrender to God in perfect obedience. Throughout the Bible, self-surrender characterizes the faithful. Abraham abandons friends and native country to go to a land unknown to him, because God called him to do so. At the voice of God, he gives up all his cherished hopes in his only son, Isaac. Moses, at the call of God, surrenders self, and in faith undertakes the deliverance of his fellow Israelites. He is willing to be blotted out of God's Book of Life, if only God would spare the people (Exodus 32:32).

2. How was Israel to express its surrender to God? Exodus 13:2, 13; 19:5-6; 22:29; Leviticus 20:7; Deuteronomy 7:6-11.

Comment: Israel itself is set apart to God as a holy people — a surrendered nation. Moreover, the entire Levitical system of sacrifice is a doctrine of self-surrender. The whole burnt offering implies the complete surrender of the worshipper to God (Leviticus 1). The law regarding the firstborn of both men and beasts emphasizes the same fundamental doctrine, as does the ritual for the consecration of priests (Leviticus 8).

3. Does self-surrender involve giving oneself? Isaiah 53:7; Nehemiah 2:5; Esther 4:16; Acts 2:44-45; 4:34-37; 20:22-24.

Comment: During their return from exile, the faithful remnant of Judah endures great hardships for the nation's future and to accomplish God's purposes. We can also see this spirit in Isaiah's prophecy of the Messiah. Nehemiah surrenders his position in Shushan to help reestablish the returned exiles in Jerusalem. Esther is prepared to surrender her life to ensure her people's safety. The early disciples, counting none of their possessions as their own, give for the good of all. Stephen and others give of themselves to the point of martyrdom. Paul surrenders himself joyfully for God's use, carrying out his commission, not knowing what dangers might lay ahead.

4. Ultimately, what does self-surrender require? Galatians 2:20; Colossians 2:20; Romans 6:6, 7; 12:1; I Corinthians 6:19-20; I Peter 2:13-17; 5:5, 6.

Comment: Our self-surrender is to die with Christ, crucifying the old man that a new man may live. In so doing, the man no longer lives for himself, but Christ lives in him. We are no longer our own, but Christ's, and by making this living sacrifice, we die daily. Consequently, we must also surrender ourselves for our neighbors' welfare and subject ourselves to those in authority and to civil ordinances for God's sake.

5. Does Christ's teaching and example emphasize that self-surrender is necessary to become His disciple? Matthew 16:24-28; Luke 9:59-62; 14:26-33; Philippians 2:5-18.

Comment: When certain disciples are called, they leave all and follow Christ. This dedication requires so complete a surrender of self that father, mother, and one's own life must be loved less than God. This surrender of self is never a loss of one's personality. On the contrary, it opens the way to true human potential.

Jesus not only teaches self-surrender but also practices it for our edification. As a child, He subjects Himself to His parents, and later, self-surrender distinguishes His baptism and temptation. Throughout a life of physical privation, He does the Father's will and not His own, refusing to use His power and standing with God even for His own deliverance. With His dying breath, He surrenders His spirit to the Father. While He is no ascetic and does not demand asceticism of His followers, He empties Himself and becomes obedient even to death. His working in us both to will and to do enables us to respond to His exhortation and work out our own salvation. Our reward for self-surrender is well worth the cost: eternal life and joy in God's Kingdom!

Lady Kadijatu Grace Ahene

PART II

Lady Kadijatu Grace Ahene

THE FRUIT OF THE SPIRIT: SELF-CONTROL

Have you ever lamented the fact that this world seems out of control? Partly because of rapid transportation and communication, events seem to occur so rapidly that they tumble one upon another. In our minds we are carried furiously along in their current, unable to conclude one event before another hammers away at us for attention.

A number of years ago, when it seemed that this world's major powers were careening pell-mell toward a nuclear showdown, we frequently heard the cry, "Stop the world, I want to get off!" Today, major economic crises have overrun several major nations, and like gigantic tidal waves they seem to be sweeping toward the shores of Western nations, which seem powerless to control their inexorable advance.

Events are not really out of control, because God is still on His throne. The Apostle Paul teaches in Acts 17:26, "And He has made from one blood every nation of men to dwell on all the face of the earth, and has determined their preappointed times and the boundaries of their habitation."

Job agrees:

> He makes nations great, and destroys them; He enlarges nations, and guides them. He takes away the understanding of the chiefs of the people of the earth, and makes them wander in a pathless wilderness. They grope in the dark without light, and He makes them stagger like a drunken man.
>
> Job 12:23-25

Does a drunken man exhibit much control? No, but in this example, God is manipulating events and men are powerless, though they try to turn aside His plans (see Psalm 2).

We are privileged to live, when events far beyond even nations to control and of vast importance to the outworking of God's purpose, are being maneuvered into position. Most assuredly, God is deeply involved. His dominion is over all creation, but for the present time, He has appointed Satan and his demons, the principalities and powers of this age, to rule over earth (Ephesians 6:12).

As we approach Christ's return, Satan has designed ways of life that are fast-paced, spiced by a complicated array of sense-appealing entertainments, fashions and gadgets, and filled with a confusing mix of educational, economic, religious and political systems. These lifestyles are in a constant whirl and lived on the edge of disaster. No one has time any more to meditate on how to gain control over his life.

Are we also allowing ourselves to be swept along on the crest of this surging tide of worldliness? Perhaps this is why Satan has created such a system.

Lady Kadijatu Grace Ahene

What Self-Control Means

In Galatians 5:23, "self-control" (temperance, KJV) is the translation of the Greek word enkrateia, which means "possessing power, strong, having mastery or possession of, continent, self-controlled"[3] Vincent's Word Studies of the New Testament adds that it means "holding in hand the passions and desires" (vol. IV, p. 168). The word, self-control, thus refers to the mastery of one's desires and impulses, and does not in itself refer to the control of any specific desire or impulse.

Self-control is comprehensive in practical application to life, but the Bible does not use the word extensively. It is implied, however, in many exhortations to obedience, submission and sinless living. The noun form is used only three times, the verb form twice (I Corinthians 7:9; 9:25) and the adjective form once (Titus 1:8). The negative form of the adjective is used three times. In II Timothy 3:3, it is translated "without self-control [incontinent, KJV]"; in Matthew 23:25, "self-

---

[3] Kenneth S. Wuest, Word Studies in the Greek New Testament, "Galatians," p. 160.

indulgent [excess, KJV]"; and in I Corinthians 7:5, "lack of self-control [incontinency, KJV]."

Another Greek word, nephalios, has the same general meaning, but it generally covers a more specific area of self-control. It is often translated as "temperate" or "sober." Even though its root condemns self-indulgence in all forms, the Bible's writers use it to refer to avoiding drunkenness.

Despite self-control's obvious importance, we should not limit our understanding of these words to merely the stringent discipline of the individual's passions and appetites. These words also include the notions of having good sense, sober wisdom, moderation and soundness of mind as contrasted to insanity.

We see a good example of self-control implied in Proverbs 25:28: "Whoever has no rule over his own spirit is like a city broken down, without walls." No specific Hebrew word in this sentence means "self-control," but "rule" certainly implies it. In its comments on this verse, the Interpreter's Dictionary of the Bible states:

The picture is that of a city whose walls have been so nearly destroyed as to be without defense against an enemy; so is the man who has no restraint over his spirit, the source of man's passionate energies. He has no defense against anger, lust, and the other unbridled emotions that destroy the personality. (NKJ Dictionary, vol. 4, p. 267)

Proverbs 16:32 shows a more positive side of self-control:

> He who is slow to anger is better than
> the mighty, and he who rules his spirit
> than he who takes a city.

Here Solomon uses an entirely different word for "rule," but the sense of self-control remains. A comparison of the two proverbs reveals the great importance of self-control as both an offensive and defensive attribute.

Undoubtedly, self-denial, self-sacrifice and self-control are inextricably linked in Christian life; each is part of our duty to God. Yet human nature exerts a persistent and sometimes very strong force away from God, as Romans 8:7 clearly shows: "Because the carnal mind is enmity against God; for it is not subject to the law of God, nor indeed can be." It is this force that each Christian must overcome. Controlling ourselves, denying human nature its impulse to satisfy its desire, and even sacrificing ourselves are necessary if we are to stop sinning as a way of life. When we add the concepts of self-denial and self-sacrifice to our understanding of self-control, we can see more easily how large a role self-control plays in the Bible.

God, the Holy Spirit and Self-Control

II Timothy 1:6-7 makes a significant statement about the importance of self-control:

> Therefore I remind you to stir up the gift of God which is in you through the laying on of my hands. For God has not given us a spirit of fear, but of power and of love and of a sound mind.

According to Strong's Concordance, the final word of verse 7 is a noun meaning "discipline" or "self-control." Most modern translations render it as "self-control," but "sensible," "sobriety," "self-discipline," "self-restraint," "wise discretion" and "sound judgment" are also used.

God gives His Spirit to us to begin the spiritual creation that will bring us into His very image. Here, Paul ranks self-control right beside seemingly more "important" attributes of our Creator, such as courage, power and love. Remember, however, that the "fruit" of God's Spirit is written in the singular; it is one fruit, a balanced package needed to make a son of God whole.

These verses tell us what kind of men God is creating: men of courage, power, and love; men who are self-governing, sensible, sober, restrained and disciplined in their manner of life. These qualities are products of God's Spirit in us. Paul adds more to this concept of self-control in Titus 2:11-14:

> For the grace of God has appeared to save all men, and it schools us to renounce irreligion and worldly passions and to live a life of self-mastery, of integrity, and of godliness in this present world, awaiting the blessed hope of the appearance of the Glory of the great God and of our Savior Christ Jesus, who gave Himself up for us to redeem us from all iniquity and secure Himself a clean people, with a zest for good deeds.

One reason God has given us grace is for us to express self-control. It is hard to imagine a Christian, preparing for the Kingdom of God, who does not strive for continual and resolute self-government, that is, one who allows his passions, tastes and desires unbridled freedom to express themselves. That is what the world does! When we witness such a demonstration, it gives strong evidence that the person is unconverted. Blind passion is not meant to be our guide. If men live guided by their animal passions, they will land in the ditch, because "God is not mocked; for whatever a man sows, that he will also reap" (Galatians 6:7).

Paul writes in Galatians 5:17, "For the flesh lusts against the Spirit, and the Spirit against the flesh; and these are contrary to one another, so that you do not do the things that you wish." Sometimes we seem to consist of a whole clamorous mob of desires, like week-old kittens, blind of eye with mouths wide open, mewing to be satisfied. It is as if two voices are in us, arguing, "You shall, you shall not. You ought, you ought not." Does not God want us to set a will above these appetites that cannot be bribed, a reason that cannot be deceived and a conscience that will be true to God and His standards? We must either control ourselves using the courage, power and love of God's Spirit, or we will fall to pieces.

Adam and Eve established the pattern for mankind in the Garden of Eden. All of us have followed it, and then, conscience-smitten, we rankle under feelings of weakness. They were tempted by the subtle persuasions of Satan and the appeals of their own appetites for forbidden fruit that looked so good. To this they succumbed, and they sinned, bringing upon themselves the death penalty and much more evil besides. What is the use of appealing to men who cannot govern themselves, whose very disease is that they cannot govern themselves? Whose conscience cries out often both before and after they have done wrong, "Who shall deliver me from this body of death?" It is useless to tell a king whose subjects have overthrown him to rule his kingdom. His kingdom is in full revolt, and he has no soldiers behind him. He is a monarch with no power.

A certain Bishop Butler said, "If conscience had power, as it has authority, it would govern the world." (Bishop David J. Butler, Christ Embassy

Ministry, 10/2015) Authority without power is nothing but vanity. Conscience has the authority to guide or accuse, but what good is it if the will is so enfeebled that the passions and desires get the bit between their teeth, trample the conscience and gallop headlong to the inevitable collision with the ditch?

The solution to this lies in our relationship with Christ:

> Therefore, my beloved, as you have always obeyed, not as in my presence only, but now much more in my absence, work out your own salvation with fear and trembling; for it is God who works in you both to will and to do for His good pleasure.
>
> Philippians 2:12-13

This is the only thing that will give us complete self-control, and it will not fail.

In Luke 11:13, Jesus makes this wonderful promise of strength to those who trust Him:

If you then, being evil, know how to give good gifts to your children, how much more will your heavenly Father give the Holy Spirit to those who ask Him!

Trust Jesus Christ, and ask Him to govern. Ask Him for more of God's Holy Spirit, and He will help you to control yourself. Remember, II Timothy 1:7 says this is a major reason that He gives us His Spirit. He will not fail in what He has promised, because the request fits perfectly into God's purpose of creating sons in His image.

Made Strong Out of Weakness

If we will only go to the Lord and trust Him with ourselves, living in true communion with Him while we patiently exercise the gifts that He gives, our lives will be in step with what Paul experienced through his "thorn in the flesh":

> Concerning this thing I pleaded with the Lord three times that it might depart from me. And He said to me, "My grace is sufficient for you, for my strength is made perfect in weakness."
>
> II Corinthians 12:8-9

In Hebrews 11:32-34, Paul recounts a few of the deeds of the heroes of faith in ages past:

> And what more shall I say? For the time would fail me to tell of Gideon, and Barak and Samson and Jephthah, also of David and Samuel and the prophets: who through faith subdued kingdoms, worked righteousness, obtained promises, stopped the mouths of lions, quenched the violence of fire, escaped the edge of the sword, out of

weakness were made strong, became valiant in battle, turned to flight the armies of the aliens.

God's love for us will fan His Spirit in us into responding in courage, strength, love and self-control. He who brought quietness and tranquility to the raging maniac, whom even chains could not hold, will give us power over the one city which we must govern – ourselves (Mark 5:1-15). We must not allow self-control to be deprecated in our minds to be of minor importance, because we are persuaded that "Christ did it all for us." Nor can we allow such a deprecation to lead us to abuse God's mercy.

Self-control is an attribute of our Creator that Jesus exemplified in His life and that Paul strongly exhorts us to exercise in ours. If we are to be made in our Father's image, we will yield to God in this matter to glorify Him with our moderation in all things and rigid resistance to sin.

THE FRUIT OF THE SPIRIT: LOVE

"What the world needs now is love, sweet love are the opening words to a popular ballad of a number of years ago. "(Hal David and Burt Bacharach, 1965) It expresses a desire that virtually everyone holds. But what is love? Judging by the commonly held understanding of "love," the world does not need any more of it! If what is happening in the world is evidence, it is very clear the world has only the foggiest of notions of what love is. If it does know, it is not doing it, or the song would not be making the statement of need.

Love is a much abused term. Because of our experiences, we all have somewhat different ideas about it. The most prevalent notion in the Western world is that love is a warm, topsy-turvy feeling, a thrill one gets in the pit of the stomach or a tingle running up and down the spine. We think of it as a warm sense of regard, a strong desire to be with or be satisfied by someone or something.

Some have equated it with caring, benevolent giving or nothing more than sheer emotionalism. On occasion, we use the term very casually and loosely. People express their "love" for the liturgy of a certain church. Some will say they just "love" ice cream, a certain beer, pizza, style of house, color, automobile, fashion, performer or team. People say they love an endless number of things. What some call "love" a theologian might call unbridled lust.

But these statements become ridiculous once we begin to understand what Biblical love is. People's "love" of something is merely an opinion, a preference. A preference is not love, and to use "love" in this way devalues it.

To care about something is not love either. One can care to the point of obsession or lust. A measure of caring must be a part of true love, but by itself, that caring feeling or preference is not love.

Love's Supreme Importance

In I Corinthians 13, the Bible reveals love's supreme importance to life. Paul directly compares love's value to faith, hope, prophecy, sacrifice, knowledge, the gift of tongues and indirectly with all other gifts of God mentioned in chapter 12. He in no way denigrates the others' usefulness to life and God's purpose, but none can compare in importance to love.

The Corinthians took great pleasure in their gifts, just as we would, but a gift's relative importance is shown in its temporal quality. That is, there are times when a gift is of no use. But love will never end; it will always be of use.

Indeed, the receiving of gifts from God – unless accompanied by and used with love – have the potential to corrupt the one receiving them. God's gifts are powers given to enhance a person's ability to serve God in the church. However, we have all heard the cliché, "power corrupts, and absolute power corrupts absolutely." If gifts are not received and used with love, they will play a part in corrupting the recipient, just as they were corrupting the Corinthians. Love is the attribute of

God that enables us to receive and use His gifts without corruption.

The Bible says in I Corinthians 8:1, "Knowledge puffs up, but love edifies [builds up]." "Puffs up," which opposed to "edifies," implies tearing down, destruction. Paul is saying that pride has the power to corrupt the bearer of knowledge. This statement is part of the prologue to the great chapter on love, written because the Corinthians had allowed their emphasis to drift into the wrong areas. Even as a gift from God, knowledge has the potential to corrupt its recipient, if it is unaccompanied by love.

Paul thus begins chapter 13 by contrasting love with other gifts of God. He does this to emphasize love's importance, completeness, permanence and supremacy over all other qualities we consider important to life and/or God's purpose.

Prophecies end because they are fulfilled. The gift of tongues is less necessary today as then, because of the widespread use of English in commerce, politics and academia. Its value depends on specific needs. Knowledge is increasing so rapidly that old knowledge, especially in technical areas, becomes obsolete as new developments arise. Yet the need for love is never exhausted; it never becomes obsolete. God wants us to use it on every occasion.

Paul also admonishes us by instructing us "to put away childish things" (verse 11), as well as his reference to a mirror (verse 12) – that love is something we grow in. It must be perfected.

What we have now is partial. Therefore, God does not give it to us in one huge portion to be used until we run out of it. In that sense, we must always see ourselves as immature, but a time is coming when love will be perfected, and we will have it in abundance like God. In the meantime, while we are in the flesh, we are to pursue love (I Corinthians 14:1).

This indicates that the Biblical love is not something we have innately. True, some forms of this quality we call love come unbidden; that is, they arise by nature. But this is not so with the love of God. It comes through the action of God through His Spirit, something supernatural (Romans 5:5).

Love, Debt and Motivation

In Romans 13:8-10 Paul injects love into the context of law, showing that it is the sum of all duties:

> Owe no one anything except to love one another, for he who loves another has fulfilled the law. For the commandments, "You shall not commit adultery," "You shall not murder," "You shall not steal," "You shall not bear false witness," "You shall not covet," and if there is any other commandment, are all summed up in this saying, namely, "You shall love your neighbor as yourself." Love does no harm to a neighbor; therefore love is the fulfillment of the law.

He does not say love ends the need for law, but that it fulfills, that is, performs or accomplishes the law.

Notice love's relationship to law in context with what immediately precedes it. The context is a Christian's response to government. He should submit to and honor human government as God's agents in managing human affairs. A Christian is indebted to the government to pay tribute and taxes. When we pay them, a Christian is no longer financially indebted to the state until it imposes taxes the following year.

Regarding men, we are not to be in debt. He is not saying a Christian should never owe anybody money, but that there is a debt we owe to every person that we should strive to pay every day. This debt is one of love! It's paid by keeping God's law and this Paul illustrates by quoting several of the Ten Commandments. Inherent in this debt is that no matter how much we pay on it each day, when we wake up the next day, the debt is restored, and we owe just as much as we did the day before!

This sets up an interesting paradox, because we owe everyone more than we can ever hope to pay. The paradox, however, is more apparent than real, because this is not what Paul is teaching. He is teaching that love must be the driving force, the motivation, of everything we do. This points out a weakness of law regarding righteousness. Law, of and by itself, provides neither enough nor the right motivation for one to keep it.

Notice in Romans 13:3: "For rulers are not a terror to good works, but to evil. Do you want to be unafraid of the authority? Do what is good, and you will have praise from the same." Laws are stated and have penalties. Rulers enforce them, but that does not stop people from breaking them, in many cases with impunity, especially if they feel no government representative is watching them. The government's power lies largely in coercion, meaning forcible constraint or restraint, whether moral or physical. In other words, it is government by force.

For instance, most people flagrantly disobey the speed limit on freeways and interstates, especially when they are not crowded, until they spot a patrol car with a trooper or two in it. Suddenly the speed limit becomes the norm, until the trooper is again out of sight. That the law is on the books, prominently displayed and is common knowledge is insufficient motivation for many people to obey.

But love toward God, as well as, the love of God, can motivate us to do what the law says to do, but cannot motivate us to do. We can conclude that Paul claims that if one exercises God's love in paying his debt to man, he will keep the commandments.

We could also conclude that Paul says that if one does not break the commandments, he is acting out of love. This is the weaker of the two minds. Within this context, then every phase, every facet of our responsibility to God and man, is covered, if we make sure love has its place as the motivation for all we do.

If we really love another person, we cannot possibly injure him. Love would immediately stifle any thought that leads to adultery, murder, theft or any form of covetousness, because love cannot harm. Since love cannot break the laws designed to protect another, it is supreme in providing the right kind of persuasion.

Love as a Bond

In Colossians 3:12-14 Paul shows another aspect of love's supreme importance to community life:

> Therefore, as the elect of God, holy and beloved, put on tender mercies, kindness, humbleness of mind, meekness, longsuffering; bearing with one another, and forgiving one another, if anyone has a complaint against another; even as Christ forgave you, so you also must do. But above all these things put on love, which is the bond of perfection.

Paul puts love "above all," showing that love is the epitome of virtues. Here, its importance is as "the bond" – something that binds or holds things together, like a congregation.

Eventually, all groups tend to fly apart. They do not remain united by magic. Generally, a group maintains its unity through a common cause. As each person contributes to attaining that cause, unity is generally served. However, even though individuals expend effort to achieve the cause, frictions arise from a multitude of reasons. Love is the supreme quality that enables the members of the group to maintain unity and keep it from flying apart. This is achieved by each person constraining or restraining himself to act in love.

Interestingly, qualities that we normally think of as being manly, like drive, courage, determination and aggressiveness, are missing from this list in Colossians 3. Though they are not inherently evil, they play directly into the human ego, frequently resulting in crass individualism.

Because it tends to produce division, individualism is not what Paul is aiming for here. Without strong spiritual control, those traits tend to descend into competitiveness, anger, wrath, malice, dissembling, accusation, slander, and foul talk. These in turn are nothing more than unashamed, self-seeking traits that split and divide.

Each virtue Paul lists is actually an expression of love, traits that make it possible to live in a community. There is nothing weak and effeminate about them: It takes a strong person to resist what comes naturally and do what God commands rather than go along with urges of our carnal feelings. Paul lists love as a separate attribute here, to show that it is not limited to the qualities he names.

Lady Kadijatu Grace Ahene

God, Man and Love

Some have called I John 4:7-12 the most sublime statement in the entire Bible regarding God's nature:

> Beloved, let us love one another, for love is of God; and everyone who loves is born of God and knows God. He who does not love does not know God, for God is love. In this the love of God was manifested toward us, that God has sent His only begotten Son into the world, that we might live through Him. In this is love, not that we loved God, but that He loved us and sent His Son to be the propitiation for our sins. Beloved, if God so loved us, we also ought to love one another. No one has seen God at any time. If we love one another, God abides in us, and His love has been perfected in us.

If we are going to be like Him, these verses are important to us, because they tell us much about Him and our responsibilities. First, love is of God – He is its Source. This love, the Apostles write about, comes from God and is not normally a part of man's nature. It is agape love. Human love, apart from God, is at its best a mere pale and vague reflection of what God is eternally.

Next, John says "God is love." Sublime as this is, some have misunderstood it because it can be misleading. God is not just an abstraction like love. He is a living, dynamic and powerful Being whose personality has multiple facets. He cannot be boxed, wrapped and presented as merely being one attribute.

John's statement literally reads, "The God is love." The Greeks used an emphatic form of writing, and here the emphasis is on the word "God." The syntax means the two words "God" and "love" are not interchangeable. "Love" describes God's nature. A good paraphrase would read, "God, as to His nature, is love." God is a loving God!

This does not mean that loving is one of God's activities, but that every activity of God is loving. If He creates, He creates in love. If He rules, He rules in love. If He judges, He judges in love. Everything He does expresses His nature. God and His nature are manifested by what He does. By love, God is revealed and known.

The very existence of life in others, besides Himself, is an act of love. His love is revealed in His providence and care of His creation. Since we are not robots, free-moral agency is an act of His love. God, by a deliberate act of self-limitation, endowed us to respond with mind and emotion. We are not animals. God's love is the explanation for redemption and our hope of eternal life. Out of love, God has given us something to live for. Life is not just a matter of going through the paces. We do not live our lives in vain.

God made humanity in His image and likeness. But the Bible says, "God is Spirit" and "God is love." Man, though, is flesh, and the Bible describes us as carnal, self-centered and deceitful. In practical fact, this means that man cannot be what he is meant to be until he loves as God loves. Only then will he truly be in the image of God, because he will have the same nature as God. So, to achieve his potential, a person must love, but he must love with the love of God.

John 13:35 adds, "By this all will know that you are My disciples, if you have love for one another." Even as God is revealed by what He does, so will His children. Our love for God has not made this possible, but His love for us, as I John 4:19 says, "We love Him because He first loved us." Thus, our love for Him is a response to His love for us. Since God shows His love for us by drawing us to Him, it behooves us to do acts of love toward others to draw them.

God's act of love in giving His Son defines the ultimate requirement of true love, the giving of our most beloved possession in sacrifice for another's gain. We can understand then, that godly love will almost always have sacrifice involved in its giving. Sacrifice is the essence, that is, the essential or vital part of love.

God's love originates in Himself, was manifested in His Son and is perfected in His people. God's love is perfected in us when we reproduce it in or among ourselves, primarily in our fellowship. We either use love and perfect it or lose it. This partly explains the Apostle John's intense concern about fellowship. What concerned him is not just an optional blessing to believers, but a fundamental outlet for the manifestation and perfection of God's love among and in the saints.

Lady Kadijatu Grace Ahene

How May We Have This Love?

It should be obvious that we neither have God's love by nature, nor is it self-generated. Romans 5:5 verifies this understanding: "Now hope does not disappoint, because the love of God has been poured out in our hearts by the Holy Spirit which was given to us." We receive godly love from its Source, God, by means of His Spirit.

Only by knowing God can we have this love, and only by loving can we know Him! This may sound like a vicious cycle, but the two go together. Only by learning to love God can we learn His nature, that is, what He is like. We cannot have that love until we first come to know Him. By fellowshipping with Him, we come to know Him and receive His love, and in using His love, we become like Him and really know Him. We can only really come to know God by experiencing the use of His love ourselves.

All this is possible because God, in His love, initiates a relationship with us, grants us repentance, gives us His Spirit, and then, because of His love, takes the lead in sustaining the relationship. This is why Paul says in Romans 5:10

that "we shall be saved by His life." He primarily shoulders the burden of our salvation. How comforting!

What Is this Love?

I John 5:1-3 is helpful in defining God's love in a practical way:

> Whoever believes that Jesus is the Christ is born of God, and everyone who loves Him who begot also loves him who is begotten of Him. By this we know that we love the children of God, when we love God and keep His commandments. For this is the love of God, that we keep His commandments. And His commandments are not burdensome.

God intends the love of Him and the love of man to be inseparable parts of the same experience. John explains this by saying that if we love the Father, we also love the child. If we love the Father, who begot the children, we must love the children, otherwise, we do not have God's love. In I John 4:20, he amplifies this: "If someone says, 'I love God,' and hates his brother, he is a liar; for he who does not love his brother whom he has seen, how can he love God whom he has not seen?"

I John 5:3 is the Bible's basic definition of love. The commandments define, make clear, what the basic elements of love are and what direction our actions should take if we would show love. This means that obedience to God is the proof of love. Obedience is an action that submits to a command of God, a principle revealed in His Word and/or an example of God or the godly.

In a sense, this is where godly love begins in a human being. Obeying God's commands is love, because God is love. Because His very nature is love, it is impossible for Him to sin. Thus He gives us commands in love, and they will produce right and good results. Any command of God reflects what He Himself would do were He in the same situation.

Jesus says in John 14:15, "If you love Me, keep My commandments." Keeping the commandments is how one expresses love. He adds in John 15:10, "If you keep My commandments, you will abide in My love, just as I have kept My Father's commandments and abide in His love."

A person may have a thought to do good or to refrain from evil. He may have a feeling of compassion, pity or mercy. One may feel revulsion about doing an evil action, but none of these become love until the thought or feeling motivates one to act. In the Biblical sense, love is an action!

Love has yet another aspect, however. We can show love coldly, reluctantly, in "dutiful obedience." We can also show it in joyous, wholehearted enthusiasm or warmhearted, thankful devotion. Which is more attractive to God or man as a witness?

Regardless of the attitude, it is far better to obey than not at all (Matthew 21:28-31). If we cannot get beyond doing what is right, the proper feelings will never be formed. Experience is largely responsible for training attitude and emotion. We will never form proper emotions without first performing the right actions with the right spirit, God's Holy Spirit.

Lady Kadijatu Grace Ahene

Coming to Know God

I John 2:3-6 helps us understand how we can have the right attitude and emotion in our obedience:

> Now by this we know that we know Him, if we keep His commandments. He who says, "I know Him," and does not keep His commandments, is a liar, and the truth is not in him. But whoever keeps His word, truly the love of God is perfected in him. By this we know that we are in Him. He who says he abides in Him ought himself also to walk just as He walked.

We come to know God through the same general process we get to know fellow human beings—by fellowshipping or experiencing life with them.

Around 500 years before Christ, Greek philosophers believed they could come to know God through intellectual reasoning and argument. This idea had a simple premise: that man is curious! They reasoned that it is man's nature to ask questions. Since God made man so, if men asked the right questions and thought them through, they would force God to reveal Himself. The flaw in this is seen in the fruit it produced. Though it supplied a number of right answers, it did not, could not, make men moral beings. Such a process could not change man's nature.

To them, religion became something akin to higher mathematics. It was intense mental activity, yielding intellectual satisfaction, but no moral action. Plato and Socrates, for example, saw nothing wrong with homosexuality. The gods of Greek mythology also reflect this immorality, as they had the same weaknesses as human beings.

A few hundred years later, the Greeks pursued becoming one with God through mystery religions. One of their distinctive features was the passion play, which always had the same general theme. A god lived, suffered terribly, died a cruel, unjust death and then rose to life again. Before being allowed to see the play, an initiate endured a long course of instruction and ascetic discipline. As he progressed in the religion, he was gradually worked into a state of intense expectation.

Then, at the right time, his instructors took him to the passion play, where they orchestrated the environment to heighten the emotional experience: cunning lighting, sensuous music, fragrant incense and uplifting liturgy. As the story developed, the initiate became so emotionally involved, that he identified himself with and believed he shared the god's suffering, victory and immortality.

But this exercise failed them in coming to know God. Not only did it not change man's nature, but the passion play was also full of lies! The result was not true knowing, but feeling. It acted like a religious drug, the effects of which were short-lived. It was an abnormal experience, somewhat like a modern Pentecostal meeting where worshippers pray down the "spirit" and speak in tongues. Such activities are escapes from the realities of ordinary life.

Lady Kadijatu Grace Ahene

God Reveals Himself!

Contrast these Greek methods with the Bible's way of knowing God. Knowledge of God comes, not by speculation or emotionalism, but by God's direct self-revelation. In other words, God Himself initiates our knowing of Him, beginning our relationship by drawing us by His Spirit (John 6:44).

What God reveals is equally important. He reveals Himself as a holy, loving and giving God with a purpose so awesome that our minds cannot grasp its full implications, though we can appreciate it. He shows that if we truly desire to be part of His awesome creative purpose, our covenant with Him obligates us to be as holy, loving and giving as He is!

God guides and empowers us in this great pilgrimage by the Holy Spirit, but obedience, following God's commands, is the way we begin to experience and grow in God-life, called "eternal life" in the Scriptures. By obedience we come to know God. It is like walking in His shoes, as it were.

In its Biblical usage, the word "know" implies intimacy. From Biblical examples, this implication can even mean sexual intimacy. That is really knowing someone closely, especially considering how long a relationship with God exists. When we apply this to our relationship with God, the sexual dimension disappears, and the intimacy becomes a deep and abiding reverence, devotion and loyalty.

People may think of God as nothing more than an intellectual exercise. They might say "I know God," or believe in a "first cause" or Creator, without having any moral compunction. They go to church on Sunday and live the rest of the week just like all their neighbors and coworkers.

People may be emotional, saying God is in them and that they are filled with the "spirit," yet fail to see God in terms of commandments. They see God as something warm and snugly, a grandfatherly figure who rushes to their aid to blow away their problems, but they do not see Him as still purposefully creating.

Unmistakably and without compromise, Jesus, Paul and John show that the only way that we can show we know God, that He is in us and we love Him is if we have been regenerated by His Spirit and are obeying Him.

Lady Kadijatu Grace Ahene

How High Is the Standard?

We can approach this question in a number of ways, but in comparing some Scriptures, the answer becomes clear as we see a pattern develop. Jesus states the second great commandment, "You shall love your neighbor as yourself." (Matthew 22:39) All by itself, this establishes a very high standard, because we love ourselves so much. We will sacrifice a great deal to please ourselves.

He raises this a notch or two when He says in Matthew 5:44, "But I say to you, love your enemies, bless those who curse you, do good to those who hate you, and pray for those who spitefully use you and persecute you." This is a great challenge, confirming that the love of God is certainly not natural to us.

Our Savior also says in John 15:13, "Greater love has no one than this, than to lay down one's life for his friends." Paul draws this standard out even further by reiterating Jesus' own example in Romans 5:7-8:

> For scarcely for a righteous man will one die; yet perhaps for a good man

someone would even dare to die. But God demonstrates His own love toward us, in that while we were still sinners, Christ died for us.

He adds in Ephesians 5:25 that we are to love "just as Christ also loved the church and gave Himself for it."

We are dealing with a love of such towering strength and determination our Lord and Savior Jesus will sacrifice himself over a long time even for his enemies. And if that is not enough, he will finally give himself totally in death for their well-being before it is reciprocated!

Will we ever live up to that? It is possible, but only because God has made us partakers of the divine nature. We now have the same Spirit in us that enabled and empowered Jesus. Peter writes:

> Grace and peace be multiplied to you in the knowledge of God and of Jesus our Lord, as His divine power has given to us all things that pertain to life and godliness, through the knowledge of

Him who called us by glory and virtue,
by which have been given to us
exceedingly great and precious
promises, that through these you may
be partakers of the divine nature,
having escaped the corruption that is
in the world through lust.

II Peter 1:2-4

Love, godly love, is the fruit, the product of that Spirit which now courses through our lives. That Spirit guides us and leads us into truth. It remains our responsibility, however, to choose to follow its guidance, to obey the truths of the great God who is creating His image in us. Obedience to His commands is godly love; the fruit of His Spirit that empowers us, the supreme virtue of the Almighty Creator.

Lady Kadijatu Grace Ahene

THE FRUIT OF THE SPIRIT: PATIENCE

Affliction, Anger, Complaining, Enduring Trials and Tests

When the Apostle Paul penned the nine qualities we call "the fruit of the Spirit," he neatly divided them into three general groups, though some overlapping of application occurs between them. The first group—love, joy and peace—portrays a Christian's mind in its most general form, with special emphasis on his relationship with God. The second group, beginning with patience ("longsuffering" in the KJV and NKJV), contains social virtues relating to our thoughts and actions toward fellow man and our attitude during trials.

The quality of patience evokes images of stoicism, tolerance and passivity in most people's mind. Though some of these elements are contained within the scope of what the Bible reveals of this very important character trait, it is far too rich in meaning to be limited to them.

We all know people who are easily irritated. They invariably let others know it, either by a steady stream of grumbling, carping or griping accompanied by a face painted with the pain of having to suffer the fools surrounding them, or they "blow up" in red-faced fury, shouting a torrent of invective intended to let everyone within hearing distance know they have been put upon and have "had it." The great bulk of us are in between. We may not show much agitation on the outside, but inwardly we are churning with varying degrees of stress, wishing that people would "just get on with it," so we can do our thing

.

Jesus and Persecution

Undoubtedly, other qualities, or lack thereof, play into these situations, but would Jesus ever act or react like this? He certainly became justifiably angry on occasion, but the Bible never illustrates Him even remotely losing control – even while under intense pressure from blinded and stubborn fools, some of whom were intentionally baiting Him. Nor does the Bible ever indicate He fell into a self-pitying pout to draw attention to His irritation.

God clearly holds Jesus up to us as the example we must strive to follow.

> For what credit is it if, when you are beaten for your faults, you take it patiently? But when you do good and suffer for it, if you take it patiently, this is commendable before God. For to this you were called, because Christ also suffered for us, leaving us an example, that you should follow His steps: "Who committed no sin, nor was guile found in His mouth"; who, when He was reviled, did not revile in return; when He suffered, He did not threaten, but

committed Himself to Him who judges righteously.

I Peter 2:20-24

Here we see patience in direct connection to our calling! Can patience possibly be that important? It is when we understand it in light of Christ's suffering for us, leaving us an example of how we are to live. We too, are called to suffer for righteousness' sake, though Peter does not limit our calling to suffering patiently.

The issue revolves around the answer to the question, "What did Christ's patient suffering produce?" Does it not follow that if Christ's life produced good things, because He lived this way, our lives will too? Did not Christ finish what God gave Him to do and glorify God in the way He did it? Does God ever counsel or command anything that does not show love and produce good?

"Many are the afflictions of the righteous," the psalmist writes in Psalm 34:19. Peter supplies a partial answer to this, as does Paul's statement in II Timothy 3:12: "Yes, and all who desire to live godly in Christ Jesus will suffer persecution." The Psalmist, Peter and Paul are all saying that persecution is a common lot – a calling – of all who strive to serve Christ faithfully.

The essence of persecution lies in subjecting the Christian to injury or disadvantage, because of his beliefs. Persecution may take many forms, but it is more than someone merely presenting counter-arguments to the Christian's convictions. It is inflicting some injury on him, putting him to some disadvantage or placing him in unfavorable circumstances.

Persecution can take on many forms within these broad areas. The injury can be to the Christian's feelings or to his family, reputation, property, liberty or influence. It may deprive him of an office or position he held or prevent him from obtaining one for which he is qualified. He could be subjected to a fine, imprisonment, banishment, torture or even death.

It follows then, that both Peter and Paul warn us that we who make a profession of Christianity must be prepared for persecution. It "goes with the territory." We are not to shrink to avoid it, but bear it patiently as Christ did.

God as Our Example

None of us has ever come close to exhibiting patience like God. Although one could not say we persecute Him as men persecute each other, yet in our own way we do bring a form of persecution on Him by our attitudes and way of life. We often live without care for His feelings about us and His creation, behaving as much of this world does, as though neither He nor His law exists.

The Bible reveals God's patience as a quality of His character that deters Him for long periods from retaliating against those who sin against Him. This fits neatly with what Peter says regarding Christ's example:

> Who, when He was reviled, did not revile in return; when He suffered, He did not threaten, but committed Himself to Him who judges righteously.
>
> I Peter 2:23

As a man, Christ did not strike back, but wisely and patiently left any retaliation due in the matter to God's judgment. This is also an example to us.

Exodus 32 contains the story of the Israelites worshiping the infamous golden calf shortly after entering into the Old Covenant with God. Soon thereafter, Moses met with God in the tent of meeting outside the camp, where he appealed to God to show him His glory. He wanted to see God with his eyes. Instead, God replied that He would make His goodness pass before him and proclaim His name.

In Exodus 34:6, when God passes before Moses, He preaches him a sermon on His attributes, fulfilling the proclamation of His name:

> And the Lord passed before him and proclaimed, "The Lord, the Lord God, merciful and gracious, longsuffering [patient], and abounding in goodness and truth."

Patience is a major characteristic of our God, and that should fill us with gratitude.

God's patience delays His wrath, allowing time for good to occur. Jonah 4:2 expresses this:

So he prayed to the Lord, and said, "Ah, Lord, was not this what I said when I was still in my country? Therefore I fled previously to Tarshish; for I know that you are a gracious and merciful God, slow to anger and abundant in loving-kindness, one who relents from doing harm."

We should also note the other qualities patience is combined with in these last two references. In combination with patience, the qualities of grace, mercy, loving-kindness, goodness and truth allow God to work with people, so they can remain alive and eventually transform into His image. If God struck out at people just as short-fused humans frequently do, no one would be alive today. Jonah, in a typically human reaction, wanted God to wipe the sinners of Nineveh, Israel's enemy, off the face of the earth!

Nineveh was undoubtedly just as full of sinners as Israel. But God, bearing patiently with them in their ignorance, sent Jonah to proclaim His warning message to them: Destruction would fall on them in forty days. They, however, believed the message, proclaimed a fast, prayed mightily to God, repented and turned from their evil ways. Their repentance may not have been Davidic, but under the circumstances God was pleased. So Jonah 3:10 records:

> Then God saw their works, that they turned from their evil way; and God relented from the disaster that He had said He would bring upon them, and He did not do it.

II Peter 3:9 affirms that God still operates in the same manner:

> The Lord is not slack concerning His promise, as some count slackness, but is longsuffering toward us, not willing that any should perish but that all should come to repentance.

Romans 2:3-6 discusses the same theme on a more personal basis, warning us that we should not abuse God's patience by viewing it as inattention, indulgence or mere tolerance:

And do you think this, O man, you who judge those practicing such things, and doing the same, that you will escape the judgment of God? Or do you despise the riches of His goodness, forbearance, and longsuffering, not knowing that the goodness of God leads you to repentance? But in accordance with your hardness and your impenitent heart you are treasuring up for yourself wrath in the day of wrath and revelation of the righteous judgment of God, who "will render to each one according to his deeds."

Solomon warns of the same perversity of nature that reveals itself in those lacking faith:

Because the sentence against an evil work is not executed speedily, therefore the heart of the sons of men is fully set in them to do evil. Though a sinner does evil a hundred times, and his days are prolonged, yet I surely know that it will be well with those who fear God, who fear before Him. But it will not be well with the wicked; nor will he prolong his days, which are as a shadow; because he does not fear before God.

Ecclesiastes 8:11-13

Clearly, God's patience is exercised so He can work on the situation and produce repentance. All too frequently though, His goodness and patience are abused through stubbornness or neglect. Be assured, God is aware, and there comes a time when His patience is exhausted and His judgment falls if the change God expects does not occur.

An Unbroken Link

In the Parable of the Unforgiving Servant, Jesus gives an interesting twist to the importance of God's patience by connecting it to our forgiveness.

> The servant therefore fell down before him, saying, "Master, have patience with me, and I will pay you all." Then the master of that servant was moved with compassion, released him, and forgave him the debt. But that servant went out and found one of his fellow servants who owed him a hundred denarii; and he laid hands on him and took him by the throat, saying, "Pay me what you owe!" So his fellow servant fell down at his feet and begged him, saying, "Have patience with me and I will pay you all." And he would not, but went and threw him into prison till he should pay the debt. So when his fellow servants saw what had been done, they were very grieved, and came and told their master all that had been done. Then his master, after he had called

him, said to him, "You wicked servant! I forgave you all that debt because you begged me. Should you not also have had compassion on your fellow servant, just as I had pity on you?" And his master was angry, and delivered him to the torturers until he should pay all that was due to him. So my heavenly Father also will do to you if each of you, from his heart, does not forgive his brother his trespasses.

Matthew 18:26-34

We desire others – especially God – to be patient and forgiving toward us in our faults, but do we practice the same attitude and conduct toward those whose faults offend us? Patience is a two-way street, and God clearly demands reciprocity. He expects us to pass His patience and forgiveness toward us on to others even as Christ did.

I Timothy 1:12-16 vividly shows Christ's example:

And I thank Christ Jesus our Lord who has enabled me, because He counted me faithful, putting me into the ministry, although I was formerly a blasphemer, a persecutor, and an insolent man; but I obtained mercy because I did it ignorantly in unbelief. And the grace of our Lord was exceedingly abundant, with faith and love which are in Christ Jesus. This is a faithful saying and worthy of all acceptance, that Christ Jesus came into the world to save sinners, of whom I am chief. However, for this reason I obtained mercy, that in me first Jesus Christ might show all longsuffering, as a pattern to those who are going to believe on Him for everlasting life.

Paul uses himself to exemplify the great magnitude of Christ's patience toward us. "Longsuffering" strongly implies forbearance under great duress. As Paul describes it, he had not just sinned in blaspheming and inflicting injury on the saints, but he had done his deeds with a proud, haughty, arrogant and insolent spirit. He acted in a wicked, malicious, violent way – a spirit of tyranny that greatly aggravated the wrong he did. Other translations render insolent as "insulter," "insolent foe," "oppressor," "wanton aggressor," "doer of outrage" and "wanton outrage."

Paul's aim is to magnify Christ's patience and forgiveness as an example to himself and his audience. The Apostle followed Christ's example by, in turn, exercising patience toward the church. Considering his own circumstance, he undoubtedly felt strongly about this, because Christ's forbearance with him opened salvation to him. In response, he passes it on to Timothy and so to us.

In II Timothy 4:2-3, Paul exhorts the Evangelist to use this virtue that means so much to our salvation:

> Preach the word! Be ready in season and out of season. Convince, rebuke, exhort, with all longsuffering and teaching. For the time will come when they will not endure sound doctrine, but according to their own desires, because they have itching ears, they will heap up for themselves teachers;

and they will turn their ears away from the truth, and be turned aside to fables.

In II Corinthians 6:3-6, the Apostle carries this thought into action, as he reflects upon his ministry and those with him.

> We give no offense in anything, that our ministry may not be blamed. But in all things we commend ourselves as ministers of God: in much patience, in tribulations, in needs, in distresses, in stripes, in imprisonments, in tumults, in labors, in sleeplessness, in fasting; by purity, by knowledge, by longsuffering, by kindness, by the Holy Spirit, by sincere love.

Twice in this listing he mentions forms of patience exercised for Christ and His people. Paul's travelling companions may very well have included Timothy, as Paul mentions him in close connection with the Corinthian church (I Corinthians 4:17; 16:10; II Corinthians 1:1, 19).

In II Timothy 3:10 he reminds Timothy:

> But you have carefully followed my
> doctrine, manner of life, purpose, faith,
> longsuffering, love, perseverance,
> persecutions, afflictions, which
> happened to me at Antioch, at Iconium,
> at Lystra – what persecutions I
> endured. And out of them all the Lord
> delivered me.

Notice that Timothy carefully followed Paul's example of patience. In Philippians 2:19-20 Paul says of him:

> But I trust in the Lord Jesus to send
> Timothy to you shortly, that I also may
> be encouraged when I know your state.
> For I have no man like-minded, who
> will sincerely care for your state.

Paul knew Timothy would regard the Philippians' interests with the same sincere tenderness and patient concern as Paul would if he were there.

Timothy followed Paul's example, Paul followed Christ's example, and Christ was One with the Father in His example. An unbroken chain of patience appears, beginning with the Father, continuing through His agent, Christ Jesus, then to His agent, the Apostle Paul, and finally to his agent, Timothy. How are we doing in continuing the chain unbroken in our relationships with others?

Lady Kadijatu Grace Ahene

Arek Appayim, Makrothumia and Hupomone

Three words are most frequently translated as either "longsuffering," "endurance," "perseverance" or "patience" in modern English Bibles: arek appayim in Hebrew, makrothumia and hupomone in Greek. When the time came to translate the Old Testament into Greek, the translators used makrothumia as the synonym of the Hebrew arek appayim. Both words mean essentially the same thing: slow to anger.

In writing the New Testament, the Apostles added hupomone. Both Greek words generally mean the same thing. However, scholars have noted that each has characteristics that sets it apart. Spiros Zodhiates, in The Complete Word Study Dictionary of the New Testament, p. 939, says:

> Makrothumia is patience in respect to persons, while hupomone, endurance, is putting up with things or circumstances.

The difference does not end there. While both words have positive connotations, hupomone tends to be decidedly more upbeat. The International

Standard Bible Encyclopedia, p. 690, says, "As makrothumia is especially related to love, so hupomone is especially related to hope." The same volume also states the distinction between hupomone and makrothumia can best be seen in their opposites. The opposite of hupomone is cowardice or despondency, whereas the antonym of makrothumia is wrath or revenge.

Thus, while makrothumia is somewhat more passive in its implications, neither word allows us to be apathetic while enduring affliction. Makrothumia is somewhat more passive because, since people are usually involved as persecutors or instruments of our affliction, we should respond with greater caution and wisdom.

People, even those who persecute us, are not things, and we best represent our Father by not being hasty and rash. "Be wise as serpents and harmless as doves," Jesus says (Matthew 10:16). It is the soft answer that turns away wrath (Proverbs 15:1). James writes, "The tongue is a fire, a world of iniquity" (James 3:6). Jesus left retaliation to the Father.

Paul says in I Thessalonians 5:15,

> See that no one renders evil for evil to
> anyone, but always pursue what is
> good both for yourselves and for all.

Two wrongs do not make a right, and in our
irritated or angry impatience, we frequently say or
do something just as bad or worse as was done to
us! Then where are we? Often, our patience does
not delay our wrath as God's does.

The obvious meaning of Paul's advice is that we
should not take vengeance. In Romans 12:19, Paul
repeats this more plainly:

> Beloved, do not avenge yourselves, but
> rather give place to wrath; for it is
> written, "Vengeance is Mine, I will
> repay," says the Lord.

This, in turn, feeds directly into Jesus' teaching in
Matthew 5:39-45:

> But I tell you not to resist an evil
> person. But whoever slaps you on your

right cheek, turn the other to him also. If anyone wants to sue you and take away your tunic, let him have your cloak also. And whoever compels you to go one mile, go with him two. Give to him who asks you, and from him who wants to borrow from you do not turn away.

You have heard that it was said, "You shall love your neighbor and hate your enemy." But I say to you, love your enemies, bless those who curse you, do good to those who hate you, and pray for those who spitefully use you and persecute you, that you may be sons of your Father in heaven; for He makes His sun rise on the evil and on the good, and sends rain on the just and the unjust.

The consistent instruction is that we not set ourselves against an evil person who is injuring us, whether verbally, physically or judicially. Rather, Jesus teaches us to be willing to give the offender something that might defuse the immediate situation—and perhaps even provide some small example that will promote his eternal welfare. Patience is of great value in this respect.

This in no way means we are weak, though to them we may at first seem so. Nor does it mean that we approve of their conduct. Though we may hate their conduct and suffer keenly when it affects us, Christ tells us to bless them, meaning we should confer favor upon or give benefits to them. We can do this by wishing the person well, speaking kindly of and to him and seeking to do him good.

Situations like this may be the most difficult test we will ever face. Patiently deferring retaliation and committing the circumstance to God's judgment is indispensable to the best possible solution. But the primary point of Jesus' instruction, however, is not how to resolve these situations, but that we may be children of our Father. By imitating God's pattern, we will resemble Him and take a giant stride toward being in His image.

Lady Kadijatu Grace Ahene

PART III

Lady Kadijatu Grace Ahene

LEARNING TO LOVE ONE ANOTHER

By this all will know that you are my
disciples, if you have love for one another.

John 13:35

In a June 2000 sermon titled "What Does God
Really Want? (Part Five)," John Ritenbaugh
expounded in relation to Romans 8:28 ("And we
know that all things to work together for good to
those who love God, to those who are called
according to His purpose"):

> All the events of life, all of the things
> that come within our possession and as
> part of our responsibility, are given to
> us for the sake of good. They are given
> to us so that through them the right
> things can be carried through the
> grave. This includes what we might
> consider bad things. Even things like
> poor health can be a good thing in
> terms of what God is doing with us,
> even though on the outside it looks like
> it's bad. If God is in your life, then even
> that sickness (though we might

consider it bad), is good. It's part of the scaffolding for building character.

From my personal experience, and from looking around the church today, it appears that many of our brethren are not being healed. It could cause us to ask, "Why is God not healing His people today?" Of course, we know that many people have been healed miraculously—and some from terrible diseases—yet others die or continue in suffering and pain.

Does this mean that the ones who are not being healed are more sinful than those who have been healed? Definitely not! If it were a matter of sin, no one would be healed, "For," as Romans 3:23 says, "all have sinned and all fall short of the glory of God." The Bible condemns all sin, so it has nothing to do with whether we have sinned more than the other fellow or not.

What then? Does God show favor to one man over another? Again, we have to turn to Scripture for the answer. In Matthew 5:45, Jesus plainly says, "He makes His sun rise on the evil and on the good, and sends rain on the just and the unjust."

God is no respecter of persons Deuteronomy 10:17; Romans 2:11

Yet, from Isaiah 53:5, we know that it is not God's intention for man to be sick: "by His stripes we are healed." This is a promise made in the present tense, making it always applicable. In addition, Psalm 103:2-3 encourages us, "Bless the Lord, O my soul, and forget not all His benefits: who forgives all your iniquities, who heals all your diseases."

We know and obey the instruction to call upon the elders when we are sick, as the Apostle James says in James 5:14 – "Is anyone among you sick? Let him call for the elders of the church, and let them pray over him, anointing him with oil in the name of the Lord."

So why are some of us not being healed?

Lady Kadijatu Grace Ahene

Working Out a Plan

We seem to be witnessing an unprecedented proportion of people who have terminal diseases. Various cancers, heart disease, diabetes, and a variety of other problems cause severe trial and discomfort to the bodies of many of our brethren, stressing and devastating them and their families too. In my personal case, as I suffer emotional pain and depression, I see the deep worry and concern – a kind of mental and emotional pain in my mother's voice as she talks to me.

Has God left us alone to suffer? Never! Being a loving God, He wants us to be well and happy; He also gives us many guidelines in His Word on how to apply His wonderful way of living, so we can be that way. But, to be painfully honest, how many of us have ourselves set these problems into motion long before we came to understand the revealed truth of God?

At one time or another in our lives, most of us have gone out and had a little too much fun. How many of us smoked for years, or drank way beyond what was good for us? We probably stayed up far too many nights burning the midnight oil, and it is likely we ate the wrong things, and to excess. There are many ways to injure the human body, and the consequences may not become apparent for many years.

Nor should we forget that some people become sick through hereditary weakness – whose fathers' sins are being visited upon them. (Exodus 20:5) For others, there is no apparent reason for their illness, and perhaps for them not knowing why, is the hardest burden to bear. God, however, lovingly supplies a means to help us to cope with the trial of disease and to grow in character at the same time. James 5:16 says, "Confess your trespasses to one another, and pray for one another, that you may be healed." Serious illness can force an afflicted person to develop a very real reliance on God. In addition, it also reveals a duty of the brothers and sisters of Jesus Christ to pray for the sick person. Why should they do this? James 5:16 continues, "The effective, fervent prayers of a righteous man avails much."

What a wonderful assurance this is for the sick church member, who may not have the strength or awareness to do much praying, although we all do the best we can at such times. Sometimes, because of pain, nausea, lack of sleep, and many other problems associated with ill health, the suffering person is not as clear-minded as a healthy person, and he is thankful that there is another who is willing to stand by him and pray for him.

All the while God is working out a wonderful plan for all of us as we stand with our brethren in sickness. Whether we are the "patient," the worried relation, or the person giving moral and spiritual support from far away, an amazing thing begins to happen: A bond – a relationship forms. And God can often work through these bonds to bring about real love, understanding, encouragement, and growth.

Lady Kadijatu Grace Ahene

Reaching Out

In I John 3:11, the aged Apostle John, the one whom Jesus loved, tells us, "For this is the message that you heard from the beginning, that we should love one another." Webster's Dictionary attempts to define Biblical love by describing it as "the fatherly concern of God for humankind and man's devout attachment to God," as well as "the unselfish, loyal, and benevolent concern for the good of another."[4]

Consider also Amos 33:33: "Can two walk together, unless they are agreed?" How does this apply to the present situation? With a unified willingness to understand and obey what Scripture demands of us as Christians, we can all walk together. Just because some are healthy (maybe they have never had an illness in their lives), does not mean they cannot try to understand and empathize with their ill brethren. With the help of God's Holy Spirit, which will make up for what any one of us lacks,

---

[4] "Love." *Merriam-Webster.com.* 2015. http://www.merriam-webster.com (8 May 2015).

the healthy can reach out and make a difference in a sick person's life.

When an individual reaches out to another who is suffering, it uplifts and encourages so much that God's Spirit has an opportunity to work with them both. Additionally, God's Spirit works to bring about comfort and a feeling of brotherhood to the ill person, and to fan the flames of loving concern in the other. These glowing embers of God's love, brotherly Christian love, help the Family of God to form fuller, deeper bonds of unity and purpose.

This is not the only way God works to cultivate His love in His people. Where there is sickness and suffering, God can take advantage of the circumstance to teach us to love each other – a command He gave to His end-time church, and to walk together as brothers. Moreover, it also provides Him the opportunity to judge who really does love the brethren.

I have made many good friends through people reaching out in loving kindness to me during my ongoing life events. I have never met most of these people, yet their love, kind words, cards, and emails keep me company in the long, lonely hours of the night. Their love has encouraged me to try a little harder the next day or has prompted me to be of good cheer and not become disheartened. It is inspiring to know that someone, a brother or sister now and in the time to come, is pulling for me and wanting me to succeed.

Above all, I know God sees these loving efforts being made and responds, pleased with our growth. He desires that we make a difference, and in reaching out, we learn to love one another and in this world, that will make an uncommon difference.

Lady Kadijatu Grace Ahene

FORGIVENESS

How important is it to forgive others? Could our eternal salvation depend on it?

There have been times in my life when I did or said something that I wished with all my heart I could take back or change. But there it was for all the world to see! Immediately, self-incrimination raced through me. I did not want to face anyone, and I wanted, if possible, to drop off the end of the earth.

Many years back, an evangelist related what he had done after making a serious mistake while speaking. Once he finished his message, he left the building, went to his car and sobbed in frustration. He was so filled with remorse and anguish that he ended up with his back on the car floor and his feet up on the seat and back rest. He truly desired things to be made right!

How wonderful it is to be forgiven for a mistake or sin! Relief floods through us. It feels as if a giant weight has been lifted from our shoulders. We may still shudder when we think about what we did, but in the next thought, we remember we have been forgiven. We really appreciate the person who realizes it was just a misunderstanding or a mistake, and says, "Hey, it's all right. Let's forget it and get on with our lives."

In looking back on our lives before being called, we begin to realize all the laws of God we have broken and that God had every right to take our life, but did not. What He did do, upon our repentance, was forgive us.

As we begin to grow in the church, sinning and forgiveness become less academic and more serious. With greater depth, we understand the sacrifice made and the price paid, so that sinning now produces greater sorrow in us. With that understanding, comes greater appreciation for the forgiveness God extends.

Forgiveness Produces Peace

Forgiveness is one of the chief characteristics we must have if we are to become literal children of God in His Kingdom. God has positions of teaching and authority prepared for us. (John 14:2, Revelation 5:10) Because these positions come with great power, we must have a heart ready and willing to forgive and forget mistakes. Those coming out of the Great Tribulation will make many mistakes, just as we have in coming out of this world. We will need to have a nature willing to encourage and forgive.

In this world it is easy to see that a major cause of conflict is an unwillingness to extend forgiveness. For example, the crisis in Sierra Leone, smoldering for many years, finally burst into flame. The rivalry between war and deadly diseases has lasted for centuries. The conflicts between churches and members, the Hatfields and the McCoys, management and labor and many others have raged with neither side being willing to forgive. At home the lack of forgiveness causes family problems to arise over and over until divorce or violence erupts.

How does God view this hardhearted lack of forgiveness? Does He take it lightly? If we lack a truly forgiving heart, could it cost us our salvation? Jesus tells us to pray:

> And forgive us our debts, as we forgive our debtors...For if you forgive men their trespasses, your heavenly Father will also forgive you, but if you do not forgive men their trespasses, neither will your Father forgive your trespasses.
>
> Matthew 6:14, 14-15

Jesus compares our sins to debts. We have violated our obligation of being obedient to God, and this exposes us to the penalty that results from that violation. To teach us the lesson of forgiveness, God bases how He forgives us by the forgiveness we extend to others!

Those who come before Him unwilling to forgive others cannot expect God to show them the love and mercy they desire. God will not show them the mercy and love they will not extend to others! If we forgive others when they injure us, our Father will forgive us.

How are we to conduct ourselves in forgiving others? We must forgive, even if the offender does not ask to be forgiven. We should treat the one who has injured or offended us with kindness, not harboring any grudge or speaking of that individual condemningly. We should always be ready to do him or her good if the opportunity arises. This is a tall order!

Why act this way when it goes so strongly against human nature? First, it produces peace. Second, it sets the example for the offending individual and for everyone else of what God considers right and proper.

Does forgiveness of a person fighting a recurring problem mean that we should place complete trust in him in the area of his problem? With many problems, i.e. poor money handling, gossip, lying, stealing and sexual sins, to name a few, we need to see a track record of overcoming before considering him trustworthy, but we can still be understanding, forgiving and encouraging.

Lady Kadijatu Grace Ahene

Forgiving a Brother

The Greek word for forgive, "aphiemi," means "primarily, to send forth, send away..., to remit" (Vine's Expository Dictionary of New Testament Words, p. 462). Vine goes on to say that it "signifies the remission of the punishment due to sinful conduct...; secondly, it involves the complete removal of the cause of the offense." It is complete pardon for wrongdoing.

Jesus instructs on the subject of offense and forgiveness in Matthew 18:15: "If your brother sins against you, go and tell him his fault between you and him alone: If he hears you, you have gained your brother." Peter, having listened to Christ's instructions through verse 20, then asks in all sincerity: "Lord, how often shall my brother sin against me, and I forgive him? Up to seven times?" (Matthew 18:21)

Peter had a definite rationale for saying "seven times." The Jews had ruled that one could only be forgiven three times, but never a fourth. Realizing Jesus would show more mercy than the Jews, he must have thought seven times was more than fair.

Christ's response shows how important forgiveness is. "I do not say to you, up to seven times, but up to seventy times seven." (Matthew 18:22) He means that we are not to limit our forgiveness to a specific number of times. As often as someone offends us and asks forgiveness, we should extend it. Further, even if he does not ask forgiveness, we should forgive him and treat him properly, setting the right example.

Then Jesus, really wanting to drive home the importance of being forgiving, tells the parable of the Unforgiving Servant (Matthew 18:23-35). The story relates how a king, settling accounts with his servants, finds that one owed him 10,000 talents. Barnes' Notes, written in the late 1800s, estimates the value at $15.8 million! Christ's point, of course, is that no one could ever repay this huge amount. Spiritually, we owe Him far more than we could ever repay.

Normally, the servant would be cast into prison and his family sold into slavery until all was paid. But when the servant entreated the king to have mercy on him, the king, "moved with compassion," forgave the entire debt!

The forgiven servant then found one who owed him 100 denarii or about $15. This petty debtor begged for additional time to pay off the debt, but the servant, without mercy, had the debtor jailed until all was paid. The king's other servants heard of this and told the king.

> Then his master, after that he had called him, said to him, "You wicked servant! I forgave you all that debt because you begged me. Should you not also have had compassion on your fellow servant, just as I had pity on you?" And his master was angry, and delivered him to the torturers until he should pay all that was due to him. So my heavenly Father also will do to you if each of you, from his heart, does not forgive his brother his trespasses.
>
> Matthew 18:32-35

We can learn several lessons from this parable:

1. Our sins are very great.

2. God has forgiven them all.

3. By comparison to the offenses we have committed against God, our families and friend's offenses against us are small.

4. We should be so appreciative of being forgiven that we freely forgive others.

5. We must forgive from the heart, not merely in words. When we truly forgive from the heart, it is as if no offense had ever occurred.

6. If we do not forgive, God is justified in not forgiving us. An example of unforgiveness in my life is when my Ex-husband would tell me, after I would say "sorry" for something I had done, "Anyone that asks for forgiveness often are wicked people."

SELF WORTH

In a brief conversation, a man asked a woman he was pursuing the question: 'What kind of man are you looking for?' She sat quietly for a moment before looking him in the eye and asking, 'Do you really want to know?' Reluctantly, he said, 'Yes. She began to expound, 'As a woman in this day and age, I am in a position to ask a man what can you do for me that I can't do for myself? I pay my own bills. I take care of my household without the help of any man...or woman for that matter. I am in the position to ask, 'What can <u>you</u> bring to the table?'

The man looked at her. Clearly he thought that she was referring to money. She quickly corrected his thought and stated, 'I am not referring to money. I need something more. I need a man who is striving for excellence in every aspect of life. He sat back in his chair, folded his arms and asked her to explain.

She said, 'I need someone who is striving for excellence mentally, because I need conversation and mental stimulation. I don't need a simple-minded man. I need someone who is striving for excellence spiritually, because I don't need to be unequally yoked...believers mixed with unbelievers is a recipe for disaster. I need a man who is striving for excellence financially, because I don't need a financial burden. I need someone who is sensitive enough to understand what I go through as a woman, but strong enough to keep me grounded. I need someone who has integrity in dealing with relationships; lies and game-playing are not my idea of a strong man.

I need a man who is family-oriented. One who can be the leader, priest and provider to the lives entrusted to him by God. I need someone whom I can respect. In order to be submissive, I must respect him. I cannot be submissive to a man who isn't taking care of his business. I have no problem being submissive...he just has to be worthy. And by the way, I am not looking for him...He will find me. He will recognize himself in me. Hey may not be able to explain the connection, but he will always be drawn to me. God made woman to be a help-mate for man. I can't help a man if he can't help himself.

When she finished her spiel, she looked at him. He sat there with a puzzled look on his face. He said, 'You are asking a lot. She replied, "I'm worth a lot."

Emotional abuse leaves few physical scars. I was a victim of emotional abuse, but I suffered no broken bones, torn flesh or spilled blood. Still, those wounds might be described as the most painful and destructive form of domestic violence.

While statistics are elusive, experts agree that emotional abuse – for mostly women, but some men as well – have reached epidemic proportions. And despite its everyday occurrence, few of us recognize it, identify it or even tried to do something about it.

By reading this, I hope it will help you learn to listen to your friends', neighbors', relatives' or maybe even your own waspish, hurtful words. And if you are a recipient of this type of domestic violence, first hold yourself in high esteem, re-evaluate your relationships and then ask for help.

There comes a critical time in each person's life when the truth is accessible. Face it, you can either run and hide denying it, or you can face your truth, accept it and grow stronger. That's what I did; it's called *Healing the Scars of Emotional Abuse.*

As you are reading this, chances are you or someone you love is in an emotionally abusive relationship. Your abuser may be a spouse, a boss, a brother or a sister. You may have tried to ignore it, deny it and fix it. Perhaps you have even tried to accept it. But it hasn't worked. This is your moment of truth. Are you willing to do what it takes to break the cycle of abuse in your life?

While the optimum situation is for both parties in an abusive situation to seek help, Dr. Tim Clinton, President of the American Association of Christian Counselors, insists one person can change the relationship. "Change a person; change a relationship," he says.

On the other hand, if the abuse is severe and occurring within the marriage relationship, it's time to take bold steps and assert Biblical, healthy boundaries.

"Sometimes separation can be a powerful attention-getting boundary if you're fully ready to use it," yes I said it! Fa Cole, who is an abuse survivor, counselor and author of *10 Lifesaving Principles for Women in Difficult Marriages states:* "The purpose of the separation can be to physically or emotionally protect you and your children or to convince your husband (or wife) that you'll not continue to live the same way. Separation can also be by mutual agreement for each to work on your own problems or demons separately with the goal of reconciling your marriage."

What follows are some general principles, gleaned from professional Christian counselors, for breaking the cycle of abuse in your life and for beginning the recovery and healing process. They are easy to understand, but difficult to implement.

Before applying these principles to your situation, it's best to seek help from the Most High, Our Father in Heaven.

Tell yourself the truth. Denial is a hallmark of abuse, which is what I was swimming in, but I invited the Holy Spirit to reveal the reality about my potential and why I stayed in an abusive relationship. When it was time, I admitted I was being abused and recognize the damage it had done.

Seeking help and guidance. There is no one-size-fits-all prescription for healing. You need the Holy Spirit to assess your situation and your safety, to help you deal with emotional baggage from the past and to help you develop a strategy for change. Healing is a lengthy and sometimes difficult journey fraught with emotional landmines. You'll need help and guidance from the Holy Spirit to walk through potentially explosive and destructive situations.

Set appropriate boundaries. In the excellent book, *Boundaries – When to Say Yes, When to Say No to Take Control of Your Life,* Dr. Henry Cloud and Dr. John Townsend, explain how and when to set appropriate, Biblical boundaries. However appropriate, set boundaries with caution; it may escalate the abuse. Experts recommend seeking professional help to guide and encourage you, but I also encourage you to seek for His presences in your life.

Find and maintain healthy relationships. It is critical to seek support from friends, family, and ideally, your church. Well not in my case I went through it all by myself with the help of the Holy Ghost.

"Pastors, church leaders and church members vary in their ability to give support to women in difficult marriages," says Downing. "Always be willing to reach out to your church for support, but remember that everybody may not have the same take as professional counselors or any human for that matter."

Support groups led by a trained professional are wonderful sources of healing and comfort. Work to build healthy, Biblical friendships and relationships. Research has shown that healthy social connections contribute to better overall health.

Soak in God's presence and truth. God invites us into his presence and transforms us by renewing our mind (Romans 12:2). Spend time in God's Word, pray, worship, and fellowship. It's possible that because you are damaged emotionally, you are unable to spend long periods of time in prayer or study. That's all right. Do what you can and trust God with the rest.

Forgive. Forgiveness is not denying or excusing the damage caused by abuse. We forgive, because God forgave us. When we forgive, we allow God to heal us. Forgiveness is a choice, not a feeling. Forgive your abuser and yourself, if necessary. God will deal with everything else.

With this help and by following these principles, you can break the cycle of abuse in your life and begin your healing journey. As you reach out to God and others, you can experience God's redemptive purposes in your life and become a channel of healing in the lives of others. Make Jeremiah 29:11 your mantra: "I know the plans I have for you, declares the Lord, plans to prosper you and not to harm you, plans to give you hope and a future."

Emotional abuse is rampant in our culture, and Christians are not immune. While all emotionally abusive relationships exact a toll on their victims, this type of domestic abuse within marriage is particularly destructive. The intimate nature of the marriage relationship presents unique challenges.

Consider YOURSELF!

I had just given birth to my daughter. Instead of brimming with joy and happiness, my relationship with my Ex was like "walking on eggshells, a time-bomb waiting to explode."

I was still in the in face of postpartum stress, my husband became angry with me. "You will have to leave this room and go into the room downstairs" he said. My heart dropped. "We don't have to be together as we planned" and he told me months later, "to live with my child and do whatever I wanted." The next day when the baby and I were in his house I said to him, "God be with you." He didn't move his lips; he looked at me and walked away...That's when I had the breakdown. I knew emotionally, I just couldn't do it anymore.

IN THE PEWS OF EVERY CHURCH, INCLUDING YOURS, ARE WOMEN WHO ARE VICTIMS OF ABUSE.

Silva is co-founder and vice president of FOCUS Ministries, Inc., one of the few Christian ministries devoted to helping victims of domestic violence and educating pastors on abuse. For Christians and non-Christians alike, the nature of domestic abuse is psychological.

"Emotional abuse is always a component of physical, sexual, and verbal abuse, but it can also stand alone," she says. "In all cases of abuse, the perpetrator uses intimidation, humiliation, isolation and fear to diminish their victim's sense of self and sanity."

Making Your Church a Safer Place

Naturally, Christians in emotionally abusive relationships, turn to their churches and pastors for help. Some feel loved and accepted unconditionally; others walk away more deeply wounded.

Dr. Tim Clinton, President of the American Association of Christian Counselors, says the impact of emotional abuse can wreak havoc on one's spiritual life.

"It's tough to believe in the fidelity of God, if all you're experiencing is ongoing abuse in your life," he says.

He challenges churches to take time to address these kinds of issues because "it deeply impacts how these women do intimacy with the Father. If our goal is spiritual vitality—spiritual growth and formation—we need to train people in how to do relationships and intimacy better."

Paul Hegstrom goes a step farther, saying that the church often turns a blind eye when confronted by someone who has been emotionally abused.

It is a sad state of affairs in the church that when a woman has been abused, it seems that the congregation, her friends, and her clergy shy away from dealing with the situation, true because I can attest to that fact. I felt forsaken by those I should be able to lean on the most. Forsaken because of an incorrect interpretation of the Scripture.

Many times in a Church world, submission is held over the heads of women by men who are emotionally drained. Do you know someone like this?

An Emotionally Abusive Childhood

My childhood was emotionally abusive and unpredictable. My mother, now a committed Christian and my hero, struggled with her own demons from her relationship with my father. There were many instances of uncontrolled rage. Not only did the incidents of her leaving to make a living frighten me, but the outbursts of rage and fear left me feeling insecure, unloved and inherently bad.

"It's your fault I act like this," I would always say.

Suicide first entered my mind at age 15. A sensitive child, I attempted to avoid my father's wrath through his absence in my life. By junior high school, weary and disillusioned, I knew thought I could never earn love and approval.

I <u>needed</u> someone's approval for everything in life, so I sought it out by lying at home, ditching studies altogether or seeking affection from the opposite sex. Lonely, insecure and feeling unlovable, I grew to accept cruel and destructive behavior from friends, thinking I didn't deserve any better.

Then I met my present Jay, a quiet, but popular friend in God. There was "love at first sight." But he had a difficult time understanding my life at first, too. Raised by both parents, hardworking father, My Jay described seeing his father as a God-fearing father, husband and friend. Jay wished to hold my hands until I felt ok. His promise filled my heart with joy.

"I will never treat you like my servant, but my helpmeet," he promised. I give God the Glory that he has kept his promise until this day.

WHY DOES REJECTION WOUND US SO DEEPLY?

Rejections attacks the very person that we are. It destroys our self-esteem, and attacks who we are and our purpose in life. This is why it is one of the most common tools the devil will use to destroy a person's life. God never wants us to feel rejected or abandoned. He desires for you to know who you really are, and realize how deeply God loves, accepts, and appreciates you, so that you can live out the fullness of what all God has ordained you to be. God's Word tells us that without being rooted and grounded in the love (and acceptance) of God, we cannot experience the fullness of God in our lives:

> And to know the love of Christ, which passeth knowledge, that ye might be filled with all the fulness of God.
>
> Ephesians 3:19

Rejection has a way of destroying a person's life in a way that few other things can. The sad fact is that the number of people who are affected by rejection is staggering. If we want to be all that God has created us to be, then overcoming rejection and its affects is vital and absolutely essential.

The Fruit of Rejection

Many people, who have faced rejection and abuse as a child, grow up with unresolved emotional wounds. Rejection causes emotional wounds, which if not cleansed and released, will grow and fester into spiritual wounds (such as unforgiveness, envy, blaming God, jealousy, etc.). Those spiritual wounds open us up to evil spirits which love to take advantage of this opportunity to invade us. The goal of the enemy is to get us built up with emotional baggage inside and negative feelings in our hearts against one another, ourselves, and God.

Rejection has a lot of fruit which can widely vary from one person to another. Some of the common symptoms of rejection include:

- Rebellion in both children and adults

- Fabricated personalities (being somebody you aren't, in order to be accepted)

- The tendency to reject others, so that you aren't the first one to be rejected

- A tendency to always wonder if a person rejects or accepts you

- The need to fit in or be accepted by others and be a part of everything

- Self-pity where a person feels bad for themselves being all alone

- Inability to be corrected or receive constructive criticism

- Rejection creates an environment where you are starved for love or just don't fit in

- A tendency to blame God ("Why did He give me this big nose? Why did God make me so short?")

- A sense of pride that says, "How dare they reject me!"

- Opinionated personality and the need to be right about things

- Feelings of worthlessness, insecurity, or hopelessness

- Seeking a parent's approval is a sign that your basing your identity upon what they think of you

- Envy, jealousy, and even hate can be rooted in rejection

- Fear of confrontation (because your identity is based upon what others think of you)

A person who has a hard time admitting they are wrong, or receiving constructive criticism has an underlying problem with rejection. How do we know that? Because they are basing their identity, who they are, upon their ability to be right about everything. Stubbornness can also be rooted in rejection, as well, for this same reason. They have to be right, or else they feel worthless... that's because "who they are" (their identity) is based upon them being right. This also ties in with opinionated personalities, who are always there to tell you all about something, even if they have little or no real understanding to speak from.

Then we have performance orientation and drivenness, certain variances of OCD, etc. where a person is basing their identity and who they are upon how well they perform at something in life. Whenever we base who we are upon our performance, or our being correct about something, and then we fail, it is a blow to our identity.

Those who struggle with rejection can also become what we call fixers; a fixer is a person who is eager to tell everybody else how they need to be doing things, but many times have little understanding or experience in such matters. Such a person attempts to be the Holy Spirit in other people's lives, where they have no authority or right to step in. They find their identity in fixing other people's problems, and they love it when people come to them for help or advice.

The truth is that we are created to be loved, accepted, and appreciated. Rejection is an anti-Christ spirit because it opposes the very nature that God created in us. Rejection starves a person from love and acceptance that they were designed to receive. The problem is that when we turn to others or even ourselves for that love and acceptance, we are setting ourselves up for failure and the damage of rejection. Only God can be trusted as the source of our identity.

Self-rejection is another piece to this puzzle. Self-rejection is where a person rejects them self. They do not like who they are. This can often lead to self-hate, self-resentment, etc. It is often tied in with self-unforgiveness, if the person has made mistakes in their life which they deeply regret. Just as it hurts when others reject us, it can do just as much damage when we reject ourselves.

Then there's perceived rejection, where a person receives something as rejection when it really isn't. For example, "Why is that person not coming over here to talk to me?" When the person may not be trying to reject you, but may just feel shy at the time about stepping out and meeting you (or anybody else for that matter). People who have spirits of rejection can have a tendency to receive perceived rejection, because the purpose of a spirit of rejection is to make us feel rejected.

A person who feels like God is always angry at them usually has issues of rejection. Perceived rejection can also make a person feel as if God has rejected them. This is a very common scene that we encounter in the deliverance ministry.

A good example of rejection, which caused feelings of envy, jealousy, and even hate to surface in King Saul can be found in 1 Samuel:

> *And the women answered one another as they played, and said, Saul hath slain his thousands, and David his ten thousands.*
>
> *And Saul was very wroth, and the saying displeased him; and he said, They have ascribed unto David ten thousands, and to me they have ascribed but thousands: and what can he have more but the kingdom?*
>
> *And Saul eyed [literally meaning that he looked with jealousy upon] David from that day and forward.*
>
> *And it came to pass on the morrow [the next day], that the evil spirit from God came upon Saul, and he prophesied in the midst of the house: and David played with his hand, as at*

other times: and there was a javelin in Saul's hand.

And Saul cast the javelin; for he said, I will smite David even to the wall with it. And David avoided out of his presence twice.

1 Samuel 18:7-11

I was reading my Bible one day, when this passage really stood out to me. First, we see the women praising David for slaying his ten thousands, but Saul for slaying his thousands. This rejection made Saul angry with David, and jealous of him. The very next day, an evil spirit came upon Saul and caused him to become exceedingly angry, to the point of attempting to murder David! Now there's some ugly fruit that all started with rejection. It wasn't rejection that opened Saul up to the evil spirit, but rather his reaction to his rejection.

The same is true when a person becomes stubborn or rebellious, or any other ungodly reaction to rejection. The rejection isn't the sin, but their reaction can be a serious sin. This can open the person up to unclean spirits, and lead them down the path of destruction. God's Word puts stubbornness and rebellion, for example, in the same category as witchcraft and idol worship!

> *For rebellion is as the sin of witchcraft, and stubbornness is as iniquity and idolatry. Because thou hast rejected the word of the LORD, he hath also rejected thee from being king.*
>
> *1 Samuel 15:23*

The Root of Rejection

The root of rejection is actually incredibly simple: damage from rejection is the result of a misplaced identity. Whenever we base our identity on somebody or something other than what God's Word has to say about us, we make ourselves vulnerable to the damage of rejection. Many of us will base our identity on what our parents, teachers, or friends think of us. This sets a lot of children up for Performance Orientation bondages later in life, because their parents give them conditional love based on their grades or performance.

What or who defines who you are? Is it your job? Is it what your parents thought or think of you? Is it what your friends think of you? Is it how well you perform in the workplace? How much money you have? Is it how good of grades you get? Is it what you think of yourself? Is it how physically strong, fit, or tall you are? When you die, will those things continue to define who you are?

Rejection and rising above rejection is all about identity and what you base your identity upon. The key to overcoming rejection is to solve the identity problems.

Let's say that you are basing your identity on what your mother and father think of you. Now the moment that any hint of disapproval comes from them concerning you, that is going to hurt because they are the source of your identity. Anytime we base our identity on what we think of ourselves, or what others think of us, we are virtually trusting that person with our identity. Not even we are capable of truly determining who we are; only God is qualified for that job. That is why it is absolutely vital for us to understand the person that God has made in us, and who we are as new creations in Christ Jesus. We were never made to live apart from God or base our identity on things of this world.

When we base our identity upon what the Word of God has to say about us, we will become virtually rejection-proof. We can become immune from the wounds of rejection as long as we are not basing our identity upon what that person thinks of us.

Some Dynamics of Rejection

The closer a person is to you, the deeper their rejection can wound you. Authority figures are also able to deeply wound you, because you look up to them and rely upon them. Parents often pass rejection on to their children when they say things such as, "I'll love you when you get good grades." Conditional love causes feelings of rejection and bondages such as performance orientation and drivenness.

Whether you love or hate a person doesn't immune anybody from rejection. You can literally want to kill somebody, but still be affected by their rejection. The question is, are you looking to them for approval? Are you basing your identity upon what they think of you? <u>Does their approval of you give your life meaning and purpose?</u>

A person's age also has a lot to do with their vulnerability to rejection. Children are especially vulnerable to the damage of rejection, because they are still developing their identity and learning about who they are. A lot of damage is done by peers in school. Either you're too short, too tall, too fat, too skinny; you have brown eyes when you should have blue eyes... you name it, and kids will pick on it! Insecure children can be very cruel and damage other children through rejection. Why? Because their own identity is not based on the right things. They do not know who they really are, or who they are called to be, so they go around putting other kids down to make themselves feel better. If they knew who they were in Christ, it would be an entirely different story! They would seek to edify other kids, and help them find their identity and calling as well.

Is it possible to receive rejection from a child or even grandchild? Yes! Nobody is immune, provided that they are basing their identity on what the other person thinks of them. You can be 100 years old, and be damaged by the rejection of a caregiver.

Get Your Identity from God's Word!

As I mentioned earlier, it is vital that we base our identity, who we are, upon what God's Word says about us. When we do, we become virtually immune from the devastating and hurtful effects of rejection. God promises never to leave or forsake us, so when our identity is based upon what He says of us, we can be assured that we're not going to face rejection coming from Him.

> *Let your conversation be without covetousness; and be content with such things as ye have: <u>for he hath said, I will never leave thee, nor forsake thee</u>.*
> *Hebrews 13:5*

So what exactly does God's Word tell us about who we are in Christ?

- Because of God's great love for us, we are adopted into His family [1 John 3:1], and made joint heirs with Christ. [Romans 8:17]

- We are made to sit in heavenly places (of authority over all demons, sickness, etc.) with Christ. [Ephesians 2:6]

- We are blessed with all spiritual blessings in Christ [Ephesians 1:3]

- We are the righteousness of Christ through faith, thus being made right before God. [Romans 3:22]

- We are entitled to a clean conscience before God because of the Blood and can have full assurance of faith when we go before Him. [Hebrews 10:22]

- Our sins have been removed from us as far as the east is from the west [Psalms 103:12], and God Himself has chosen not to remember our failures. [Hebrews 8:12]

- We are loved with the same love that the Father has for Jesus Himself! [John 17:23]

I could go on and on, because the Word of God is so rich and powerful in helping us define who we are in Christ. One of my favorite books to recommend when it comes to this subject is Victory over Darkness by Neil T. Anderson. His book on this subject is an incredible tool to change the way we see ourselves through the eyes of God's Word.

There's one verse in Psalms that really puts the light on how we can be freed from the devastating effects of rejection:

> *When my father and my mother forsake me, then the LORD will take me up.*
> *Psalms 27:10*

Overcoming religious strongholds is also necessary to overcome the effects of rejection. You're not going to settle rejection issues fully until you get it down into your spirit that you are accepted, loved, and appreciated by God. Dealing with religious strongholds is vital to this process, as religion paints God as distant, cold, and impersonal. Bringing your relationship with God into proper perspective is a vital step in the process of overcoming the strongholds of rejection.

Tearing down the strongholds of rejection is as simple as merely receiving, with childlike faith, what God's Word has to say about your identity, who you are as a new creature in Christ, who is called to life, purpose, and meaning in Christ.

FACTORS FOR HEALING

Intentional rejection is basically emotional abuse in its most simple form. It wounds a person's spirit, sometimes slightly, other times these wounds can be deep and very painful. These wounds must be healed, and here is how my wounds were healed. My spiritual mother said me, "Child, the healing process can be painful, but very helpful."

- And so I cried
- And I screamed
- I subdued by myself
- And I asked God to take total control of me.
- I fasted and prayed for inner peace.

The one thing that you absolutely cannot overlook is correcting your identity. You need to start seeing yourself for who you are in Christ, and the person that God has really formed within you. Your identity must come from Him and what His Word says about you. Printing out lists of Bible verses which speak of who you are in Christ are incredible tools to help renew your mind and tear down these strongholds. In the healing process of rejection, many times strongholds need to be torn down. Some helpful tips from Iyanla Vanzant[5] include:

- Who we REALLY are
- It's vital to love yourself!
- What's on your mind?
- The power of your thoughts
- Anti-stronghold Bible verses (print these out and speak them aloud daily!)
- How God sees us
- A Thankful Heart
- A Love Relationship w/Jesus
- Blessing Confessions (print these out and speak them aloud daily!)
- The Forgiven sinner or saint?

The Holy Spirit has shown me that whenever we feel the hurt and pain from rejection, it's because our identity depends upon what the other person thinks of us. If our identity didn't depend on what others think of us, we would

---

[5] "Life Lessons." Own Network. February 24, 2015

be virtually immune from the damage of rejection. That is why our identity must be based upon the Word of God, and what God has to say about us. This is the unshakable rock to which we need to build our house upon.

The wounds of rejection can open a person up to spirits such as abandonment, rejection, worthlessness, etc. Rejection is an open door to a wide variety of bondages, such as performance orientation, drivenness, rebellion, etc. Those who have ongoing struggles with rejection should go through the deliverance process to have those spirits removed.

Lack of love as a child, for example, can cause that child to turn to pornography and lust to fulfill their need to be loved, which then results in unloving spirits, lust, pornography, etc. to deal with. As with abuse, it's not so much the rejection that opens us up to unclean spirits, but rather our reaction to the rejection. As previously stated, true rejection is just an emotional form of abuse.

God spoke to me one time and said, "How is your heart towards that person who has rejected you? Do you love them as I have commanded you?" Forgiving the person who has rejected us is a vital step in the healing process. If we want God's help in this process, then forgiveness is not an option. Sometimes we even have to forgive God in cases of perceived rejection, such as "Why did God give me this big nose? Or this short body?" I've even struggled with unforgiveness against God, because I thought He was just too hard to please, which was a result of a religious bondage. Religion, as with so many other things, can also tie in with rejection bondages.

Today, I reach out to other women, sharing my testimony of God's faithfulness and love. I am still marveled that God has redeemed my pain and uses it to bring healing to others. God bless you as you read this book.

ACKNOWLEDGEMENTS

First and foremost I'd like to thank God for this vision. In the process of putting this book together, I realized how true His love is for mankind. To my husband **Joseph Ahene**: what can I say? Words can't express how grateful I am for you in my life. Thanks for coming up, pushing me when I almost gave up. For all the good that comes out of this book, I look forward to sharing with you. You are my hero, for you made me believe in me. I thank God for you and I love you always & forever!

To my daughters **Lois Affia Ahene & Abigail Naa-Ayeley Ahene**: you are the best thing I have ever done in life. You welcomed me into motherhood; I am so grateful for you in my life's journey, love mommy.

To the women I looked up to growing up: my biological mother, **Lucinda Katta**, her sister who made it possible for me to be in the States today, **Lucy Katta-Magona**, and to their eldest sister whom I call Mommy who took care of me from birth to 8 years old, **Mrs. Elizabeth Katta**. I can barely find words to express all the wisdom love and support you showed me all these years. All of those attributes has added up to who I am today as a woman and a mother. And to my sister **Fati .k. Samura**, I am thankful and am grateful for you all in my life.

To the sponsors, friends, and my Ministry: I could never have done this without the faith you have in me. Thank you.

BIOGRAPHY

Kadijatu E. Kamara was born in June 29, 1985 in Sierra Leone, West Africa. Her mother, Lucinda Katta and father, Abdurrahman Kamara raised their daughter to fear God. They instilled in her respect and motivation to thrive with the emphasis to succeed. Kadijatu is a motivated, classic, energetic and talented young woman that when you see her she always has a smile on her face to welcome you.

Growing up in Sierra Leone, she attended Meriwether Preparatory, Ronsabs and Freetown Secondary School for Girls. In the early 2000's she traveled to the United States and furthered her education at Glendale High school in Arizona. Kadijatu graduated with a scholarship from the GLODEN WHEEL ORGANIZATION, and was admitted at Grand Canyon University but later moved out of states to further her Bachelor's in Humanity & Social Science at Lorenzo University.

Though education is a factor to Kadijatu, she takes pride in giving back to the community. She volunteers at Community Action Council where she received an award for volunteer of the month. Her other accomplishments are: Miss teen Arizona beauty pageant contestants in 2005, modeling with SIASOLMONS FASHION DESIGNS. She was the first black young gospel artist to be on the AURGURSLEADERS NEWS PAPPER in Sioux Falls South Dakota for her unwavering efforts to organize a Christmas concert for the children; her inspiration for the concert came after the birth of her daughter Saldija Lois.

Between her schedule of hosting events or working with top musicians and movie producers/directors, Kadijatu still finds time for family and friends, she managed to get in the studio and work on her Gospel Music. She has been a wonder woman since 2006 when Kadijatu was asked by her dance teacher to sing the United States national Anthem at the Phoenix Suns game; she has been taking over the stage every time she opens her lungs to sing.

Be that as it may, the road to success for Kadijatu hasn't been easy, but she never gave up on herself. She is multi-talented in the performing arts of dancing, singing, acting and fashion and for her the sky is the limit. Her fear of God has kept her sane and humble throughout her struggles in life, but she never gave up as she continues to strive for positivity and success in her life.

www.ingramcontent.com/pod-product-compliance
Lightning Source LLC
Chambersburg PA
CBHW051832090426
42736CB00011B/1762